A COURSE IN MIRACLES®

MANUAL FOR TEACHERS

FOUNDATION FOR INNER PEACE

Published by the Foundation for Inner Peace
P.O. Box 1104
Glen Ellen, CA 95442

A COURSE IN MIRACLES was first published in three volumes in June 1976.
Second Edition
Manufactured in the United States of America

ISBN   0-9606388-7-3
Library of Congress Catalog Card Number 76-20363

94 95 96—10 9 8 7 6 5 4 3 2

CONTENTS

MANUAL FOR TEACHERS

CLARIFICATION OF TERMS

MANUAL FOR TEACHERS

INTRODUCTION

1. The role of teaching and learning is actually reversed in the thinking of the world. ²The reversal is characteristic. ³It seems as if the teacher and the learner are separated, the teacher giving something to the learner rather than to himself. ⁴Further, the act of teaching is regarded as a special activity, in which one engages only a relatively small proportion of one's time. ⁵The course, on the other hand, emphasizes that to teach *is* to learn, so that teacher and learner are the same. ⁶It also emphasizes that teaching is a constant process; it goes on every moment of the day, and continues into sleeping thoughts as well.

2. To teach is to demonstrate. ²There are only two thought systems, and you demonstrate that you believe one or the other is true all the time. ³From your demonstration others learn, and so do you. ⁴The question is not whether you will teach, for in that there is no choice. ⁵The purpose of the course might be said to provide you with a means of choosing what you want to teach on the basis of what you want to learn. ⁶You cannot give to someone else, but only to yourself, and this you learn through teaching. ⁷Teaching is but a call to witnesses to attest to what you believe. ⁸It is a method of conversion. ⁹This is not done by words alone. ¹⁰Any situation must be to you a chance to teach others what you are, and what they are to you. ¹¹No more than that, but also never less.

3. The curriculum you set up is therefore determined exclusively by what you think you are, and what you believe the relationship of others is to you. ²In the formal teaching situation, these questions may be totally unrelated to what you think you are teaching. ³Yet it is impossible not to use the content of any situation on behalf of what you really teach, and therefore really learn. ⁴To this the verbal content of your teaching is quite irrelevant. ⁵It may coincide with it, or it may not. ⁶It is the teaching underlying what you say that teaches you. ⁷Teaching but reinforces what you believe about yourself. ⁸Its fundamental purpose is to diminish self-doubt. ⁹This does not mean that the self you are trying to protect is real. ¹⁰But it does mean that the self you think is real is what you teach.

4. This is inevitable. ²There is no escape from it. ³How could it be otherwise? ⁴Everyone who follows the world's curriculum, and

1

everyone here does follow it until he changes his mind, teaches solely to convince himself that he is what he is not. ⁵Herein is the purpose of the world. ⁶What else, then, would its curriculum be? ⁷Into this hopeless and closed learning situation, which teaches nothing but despair and death, God sends His teachers. ⁸And as they teach His lessons of joy and hope, their learning finally becomes complete.

5.   Except for God's teachers there would be little hope of salvation, for the world of sin would seem forever real. ²The self-deceiving must deceive, for they must teach deception. ³And what else is hell? ⁴This is a manual for the teachers of God. ⁵They are not perfect, or they would not be here. ⁶Yet it is their mission to become perfect here, and so they teach perfection over and over, in many, many ways, until they have learned it. ⁷And then they are seen no more, although their thoughts remain a source of strength and truth forever. ⁸Who are they? ⁹How are they chosen? ¹⁰What do they do? ¹¹How can they work out their own salvation and the salvation of the world? ¹²This manual attempts to answer these questions.

1. WHO ARE GOD'S TEACHERS?

1. A teacher of God is anyone who chooses to be one. ²His qualifications consist solely in this; somehow, somewhere he has made a deliberate choice in which he did not see his interests as apart from someone else's. ³Once he has done that, his road is established and his direction is sure. ⁴A light has entered the darkness. ⁵It may be a single light, but that is enough. ⁶He has entered an agreement with God even if he does not yet believe in Him. ⁷He has become a bringer of salvation. ⁸He has become a teacher of God.

2. They come from all over the world. ²They come from all religions and from no religion. ³They are the ones who have answered. ⁴The Call is universal. ⁵It goes on all the time everywhere. ⁶It calls for teachers to speak for It and redeem the world. ⁷Many hear It, but few will answer. ⁸Yet it is all a matter of time. ⁹Everyone will answer in the end, but the end can be a long, long way off. ¹⁰It is because of this that the plan of the teachers was established. ¹¹Their function is to save time. ¹²Each one begins as a single light, but with the Call at its center it is a light that cannot be limited. ¹³And each one saves a thousand years of time as the world judges it. ¹⁴To the Call Itself time has no meaning.

3. There is a course for every teacher of God. ²The form of the course varies greatly. ³So do the particular teaching aids involved. ⁴But the content of the course never changes. ⁵Its central theme is always, "God's Son is guiltless, and in his innocence is his salvation." ⁶It can be taught by actions or thoughts; in words or soundlessly; in any language or in no language; in any place or time or manner. ⁷It does not matter who the teacher was before he heard the Call. ⁸He has become a savior by his answering. ⁹He has seen someone else as himself. ¹⁰He has therefore found his own salvation and the salvation of the world. ¹¹In his rebirth is the world reborn.

4. This is a manual for a special curriculum, intended for teachers of a special form of the universal course. ²There are many thousands of other forms, all with the same outcome. ³They merely save time. ⁴Yet it is time alone that winds on wearily, and the world is very tired now. ⁵It is old and worn and without hope. ⁶There was never a question of outcome, for what can change the Will of God? ⁷But time, with its illusions of change and death,

wears out the world and all things in it. [8]Yet time has an ending, and it is this that the teachers of God are appointed to bring about. [9]For time is in their hands. [10]Such was their choice, and it is given them.

2. WHO ARE THEIR PUPILS?

1.   Certain pupils have been assigned to each of God's teachers, and they will begin to look for him as soon as he has answered the Call. ²They were chosen for him because the form of the universal curriculum that he will teach is best for them in view of their level of understanding. ³His pupils have been waiting for him, for his coming is certain. ⁴Again, it is only a matter of time. ⁵Once he has chosen to fulfill his role, they are ready to fulfill theirs. ⁶Time waits on his choice, but not on whom he will serve. ⁷When he is ready to learn, the opportunities to teach will be provided for him.

2.   In order to understand the teaching-learning plan of salvation, it is necessary to grasp the concept of time that the course sets forth. ²Atonement corrects illusions, not truth. ³Therefore, it corrects what never was. ⁴Further, the plan for this correction was established and completed simultaneously, for the Will of God is entirely apart from time. ⁵So is all reality, being of Him. ⁶The instant the idea of separation entered the mind of God's Son, in that same instant was God's Answer given. ⁷In time this happened very long ago. ⁸In reality it never happened at all.

3.   The world of time is the world of illusion. ²What happened long ago seems to be happening now. ³Choices made long since appear to be open; yet to be made. ⁴What has been learned and understood and long ago passed by is looked upon as a new thought, a fresh idea, a different approach. ⁵Because your will is free you can accept what has already happened at any time you choose, and only then will you realize that it was always there. ⁶As the course emphasizes, you are not free to choose the curriculum, or even the form in which you will learn it. ⁷You are free, however, to decide when you want to learn it. ⁸And as you accept it, it is already learned.

4.   Time really, then, goes backward to an instant so ancient that it is beyond all memory, and past even the possibility of remembering. ²Yet because it is an instant that is relived again and again and still again, it seems to be now. ³And thus it is that pupil and teacher seem to come together in the present, finding each other as if they had not met before. ⁴The pupil comes at the right time to the right place. ⁵This is inevitable, because he made the right choice in that ancient instant which he now relives. ⁶So has the

teacher, too, made an inevitable choice out of an ancient past. [7]God's Will in everything but seems to take time in the working-out. [8]What could delay the power of eternity?

5.　When pupil and teacher come together, a teaching-learning situation begins. [2]For the teacher is not really the one who does the teaching. [3]God's Teacher speaks to any two who join together for learning purposes. [4]The relationship is holy because of that purpose, and God has promised to send His Spirit into any holy relationship. [5]In the teaching-learning situation, each one learns that giving and receiving are the same. [6]The demarcations they have drawn between their roles, their minds, their bodies, their needs, their interests, and all the differences they thought separated them from one another, fade and grow dim and disappear. [7]Those who would learn the same course share one interest and one goal. [8]And thus he who was the learner becomes a teacher of God himself, for he has made the one decision that gave his teacher to him. [9]He has seen in another person the same interests as his own.

3. WHAT ARE THE LEVELS OF TEACHING?

1.   The teachers of God have no set teaching level. ²Each teaching-learning situation involves a different relationship at the beginning, although the ultimate goal is always the same; to make of the relationship a holy relationship, in which both can look upon the Son of God as sinless. ³There is no one from whom a teacher of God cannot learn, so there is no one whom he cannot teach. ⁴However, from a practical point of view he cannot meet everyone, nor can everyone find him. ⁵Therefore, the plan includes very specific contacts to be made for each teacher of God. ⁶There are no accidents in salvation. ⁷Those who are to meet will meet, because together they have the potential for a holy relationship. ⁸They are ready for each other.

2.   The simplest level of teaching appears to be quite superficial. ²It consists of what seem to be very casual encounters; a "chance" meeting of two apparent strangers in an elevator, a child who is not looking where he is going running into an adult "by chance," two students "happening" to walk home together. ³These are not chance encounters. ⁴Each of them has the potential for becoming a teaching-learning situation. ⁵Perhaps the seeming strangers in the elevator will smile to one another, perhaps the adult will not scold the child for bumping into him; perhaps the students will become friends. ⁶Even at the level of the most casual encounter, it is possible for two people to lose sight of separate interests, if only for a moment. ⁷That moment will be enough. ⁸Salvation has come.

3.   It is difficult to understand that levels of teaching the universal course is a concept as meaningless in reality as is time. ²The illusion of one permits the illusion of the other. ³In time, the teacher of God seems to begin to change his mind about the world with a single decision, and then learns more and more about the new direction as he teaches it. ⁴We have covered the illusion of time already, but the illusion of levels of teaching seems to be something different. ⁵Perhaps the best way to demonstrate that these levels cannot exist is simply to say that any level of the teaching-learning situation is part of God's plan for Atonement, and His plan can have no levels, being a reflection of His Will. ⁶Salvation is always ready and always there. ⁷God's teachers work at different levels, but the result is always the same.

4.   Each teaching-learning situation is maximal in the sense that

each person involved will learn the most that he can from the other person at that time. ²In this sense, and in this sense only, we can speak of levels of teaching. ³Using the term in this way, the second level of teaching is a more sustained relationship, in which, for a time, two people enter into a fairly intense teaching-learning situation and then appear to separate. ⁴As with the first level, these meetings are not accidental, nor is what appears to be the end of the relationship a real end. ⁵Again, each has learned the most he can at the time. ⁶Yet all who meet will someday meet again, for it is the destiny of all relationships to become holy. ⁷God is not mistaken in His Son.

5.   The third level of teaching occurs in relationships which, once they are formed, are lifelong. ²These are teaching-learning situations in which each person is given a chosen learning partner who presents him with unlimited opportunities for learning. ³These relationships are generally few, because their existence implies that those involved have reached a stage simultaneously in which the teaching-learning balance is actually perfect. ⁴This does not mean that they necessarily recognize this; in fact, they generally do not. ⁵They may even be quite hostile to each other for some time, and perhaps for life. ⁶Yet should they decide to learn it, the perfect lesson is before them and can be learned. ⁷And if they decide to learn that lesson, they become the saviors of the teachers who falter and may even seem to fail. ⁸No teacher of God can fail to find the Help he needs.

4. WHAT ARE THE CHARACTERISTICS OF GOD'S TEACHERS?

1.   The surface traits of God's teachers are not at all alike. ²They do not look alike to the body's eyes, they come from vastly different backgrounds, their experiences of the world vary greatly, and their superficial "personalities" are quite distinct. ³Nor, at the beginning stages of their functioning as teachers of God, have they as yet acquired the deeper characteristics that will establish them as what they are. ⁴God gives special gifts to His teachers, because they have a special role in His plan for Atonement. ⁵Their specialness is, of course, only temporary; set in time as a means of leading out of time. ⁶These special gifts, born in the holy relationship toward which the teaching-learning situation is geared, become characteristic of all teachers of God who have advanced in their own learning. ⁷In this respect they are all alike.

2.   All differences among the Sons of God are temporary. ²Nevertheless, in time it can be said that the advanced teachers of God have the following characteristics:

I. Trust

1.   This is the foundation on which their ability to fulfill their function rests. ²Perception is the result of learning. ³In fact, perception *is* learning, because cause and effect are never separated. ⁴The teachers of God have trust in the world, because they have learned it is not governed by the laws the world made up. ⁵It is governed by a Power That is *in* them but not *of* them. ⁶It is this Power That keeps all things safe. ⁷It is through this Power that the teachers of God look on a forgiven world.

2.   When this Power has once been experienced, it is impossible to trust one's own petty strength again. ²Who would attempt to fly with the tiny wings of a sparrow when the mighty power of an eagle has been given him? ³And who would place his faith in the shabby offerings of the ego when the gifts of God are laid before him? ⁴What is it that induces them to make the shift?

A. Development of Trust

3.   First, they must go through what might be called "a period of undoing." ²This need not be painful, but it usually is so experienced. ³It seems as if things are being taken away, and it is rarely understood initially that their lack of value is merely being recognized. ⁴How can lack of value be perceived unless the perceiver is in a position where he must see things in a different light? ⁵He is not yet at a point at which he can make the shift entirely internally. ⁶And so the plan will sometimes call for changes in what seem to be external circumstances. ⁷These changes are always helpful. ⁸When the teacher of God has learned that much, he goes on to the second stage.

4.   Next, the teacher of God must go through "a period of sorting out." ²This is always somewhat difficult because, having learned that the changes in his life are always helpful, he must now decide all things on the basis of whether they increase the helpfulness or hamper it. ³He will find that many, if not most of the things he valued before will merely hinder his ability to transfer what he has learned to new situations as they arise. ⁴Because he has valued what is really valueless, he will not generalize the lesson for fear of loss and sacrifice. ⁵It takes great learning to understand that all things, events, encounters and circumstances are helpful. ⁶It is only to the extent to which they are helpful that any degree of reality should be accorded them in this world of illusion. ⁷The word "value" can apply to nothing else.

5.   The third stage through which the teacher of God must go can be called "a period of relinquishment." ²If this is interpreted as giving up the desirable, it will engender enormous conflict. ³Few teachers of God escape this distress entirely. ⁴There is, however, no point in sorting out the valuable from the valueless unless the next obvious step is taken. ⁵Therefore, the period of overlap is apt to be one in which the teacher of God feels called upon to sacrifice his own best interests on behalf of truth. ⁶He has not realized as yet how wholly impossible such a demand would be. ⁷He can learn this only as he actually does give up the valueless. ⁸Through this, he learns that where he anticipated grief, he finds a happy lightheartedness instead; where he thought something was asked of him, he finds a gift bestowed on him.

6.   Now comes "a period of settling down." ²This is a quiet time, in which the teacher of God rests a while in reasonable peace. ³Now

he consolidates his learning. ⁴Now he begins to see the transfer value of what he has learned. ⁵Its potential is literally staggering, and the teacher of God is now at the point in his progress at which he sees in it his whole way out. ⁶"Give up what you do not want, and keep what you do." ⁷How simple is the obvious! ⁸And how easy to do! ⁹The teacher of God needs this period of respite. ¹⁰He has not yet come as far as he thinks. ¹¹Yet when he is ready to go on, he goes with mighty companions beside him. ¹²Now he rests a while, and gathers them before going on. ¹³He will not go on from here alone.

7. The next stage is indeed "a period of unsettling." ²Now must the teacher of God understand that he did not really know what was valuable and what was valueless. ³All that he really learned so far was that he did not want the valueless, and that he did want the valuable. ⁴Yet his own sorting out was meaningless in teaching him the difference. ⁵The idea of sacrifice, so central to his own thought system, had made it impossible for him to judge. ⁶He thought he learned willingness, but now he sees that he does not know what the willingness is for. ⁷And now he must attain a state that may remain impossible to reach for a long, long time. ⁸He must learn to lay all judgment aside, and ask only what he really wants in every circumstance. ⁹Were not each step in this direction so heavily reinforced, it would be hard indeed!

8. And finally, there is "a period of achievement." ²It is here that learning is consolidated. ³Now what was seen as merely shadows before become solid gains, to be counted on in all "emergencies" as well as tranquil times. ⁴Indeed, the tranquility is their result; the outcome of honest learning, consistency of thought and full trans-fer. ⁵This is the stage of real peace, for here is Heaven's state fully reflected. ⁶From here, the way to Heaven is open and easy. ⁷In fact, it is here. ⁸Who would "go" anywhere, if peace of mind is already complete? ⁹And who would seek to change tranquility for some-thing more desirable? ¹⁰What could be more desirable than this?

II. Honesty

1. All other traits of God's teachers rest on trust. ²Once that has been achieved, the others cannot fail to follow. ³Only the trusting can afford honesty, for only they can see its value. ⁴Honesty does not apply only to what you say. ⁵The term actually means consis-tency. ⁶There is nothing you say that contradicts what you think

or do; no thought opposes any other thought; no act belies your word; and no word lacks agreement with another. ⁷Such are the truly honest. ⁸At no level are they in conflict with themselves. ⁹Therefore it is impossible for them to be in conflict with anyone or anything.

2.   The peace of mind which the advanced teachers of God experience is largely due to their perfect honesty. ²It is only the wish to deceive that makes for war. ³No one at one with himself can even conceive of conflict. ⁴Conflict is the inevitable result of self-deception, and self-deception is dishonesty. ⁵There is no challenge to a teacher of God. ⁶Challenge implies doubt, and the trust on which God's teachers rest secure makes doubt impossible. ⁷Therefore they can only succeed. ⁸In this, as in all things, they are honest. ⁹They can only succeed, because they never do their will alone. ¹⁰They choose for all mankind; for all the world and all things in it; for the unchanging and unchangeable beyond appearances; and for the Son of God and his Creator. ¹¹How could they not succeed? ¹²They choose in perfect honesty, sure of their choice as of themselves.

III. Tolerance

1.   God's teachers do not judge. ²To judge is to be dishonest, for to judge is to assume a position you do not have. ³Judgment without self-deception is impossible. ⁴Judgment implies that you have been deceived in your brothers. ⁵How, then, could you not have been deceived in yourself? ⁶Judgment implies a lack of trust, and trust remains the bedrock of the teacher of God's whole thought system. ⁷Let this be lost, and all his learning goes. ⁸Without judgment are all things equally acceptable, for who could judge otherwise? ⁹Without judgment are all men brothers, for who is there who stands apart? ¹⁰Judgment destroys honesty and shatters trust. ¹¹No teacher of God can judge and hope to learn.

IV. Gentleness

1.   Harm is impossible for God's teachers. ²They can neither harm nor be harmed. ³Harm is the outcome of judgment. ⁴It is the dishonest act that follows a dishonest thought. ⁵It is a verdict of

guilt upon a brother, and therefore on oneself. 6It is the end of peace and the denial of learning. 7It demonstrates the absence of God's curriculum, and its replacement by insanity. 8No teacher of God but must learn,—and fairly early in his training,—that harmfulness completely obliterates his function from his awareness. 9It will make him confused, fearful, angry and suspicious. 10It will make the Holy Spirit's lessons impossible to learn. 11Nor can God's Teacher be heard at all, except by those who realize that harm can actually achieve nothing. 12No gain can come of it.

2. Therefore, God's teachers are wholly gentle. 2They need the strength of gentleness, for it is in this that the function of salvation becomes easy. 3To those who would do harm, it is impossible. 4To those to whom harm has no meaning, it is merely natural. 5What choice but this has meaning to the sane? 6Who chooses hell when he perceives a way to Heaven? 7And who would choose the weakness that must come from harm in place of the unfailing, all-encompassing and limitless strength of gentleness? 8The might of God's teachers lies in their gentleness, for they have understood their evil thoughts came neither from God's Son nor his Creator. 9Thus did they join their thoughts with Him Who is their Source. 10And so their will, which always was His Own, is free to be itself.

V. Joy

1. Joy is the inevitable result of gentleness. 2Gentleness means that fear is now impossible, and what could come to interfere with joy? 3The open hands of gentleness are always filled. 4The gentle have no pain. 5They cannot suffer. 6Why would they not be joyous? 7They are sure they are beloved and must be safe. 8Joy goes with gentleness as surely as grief attends attack. 9God's teachers trust in Him. 10And they are sure His Teacher goes before them, making sure no harm can come to them. 11They hold His gifts and follow in His way, because God's Voice directs them in all things. 12Joy is their song of thanks. 13And Christ looks down on them in thanks as well. 14His need of them is just as great as theirs of Him. 15How joyous it is to share the purpose of salvation!

VI. Defenselessness

1.   God's teachers have learned how to be simple. ²They have no dreams that need defense against the truth. ³They do not try to make themselves. ⁴Their joy comes from their understanding Who created them. ⁵And does what God created need defense? ⁶No one can become an advanced teacher of God until he fully understands that defenses are but foolish guardians of mad illusions. ⁷The more grotesque the dream, the fiercer and more powerful its defenses seem to be. ⁸Yet when the teacher of God finally agrees to look past them, he finds that nothing was there. ⁹Slowly at first he lets himself be undeceived. ¹⁰But he learns faster as his trust increases. ¹¹It is not danger that comes when defenses are laid down. ¹²It is safety. ¹³It is peace. ¹⁴It is joy. ¹⁵And it is God.

VII. Generosity

1.   The term generosity has special meaning to the teacher of God. ²It is not the usual meaning of the word; in fact, it is a meaning that must be learned and learned very carefully. ³Like all the other attributes of God's teachers this one rests ultimately on trust, for without trust no one can be generous in the true sense. ⁴To the world, generosity means "giving away" in the sense of "giving up." ⁵To the teachers of God, it means giving away in order to keep. ⁶This has been emphasized throughout the text and the workbook, but it is perhaps more alien to the thinking of the world than many other ideas in our curriculum. ⁷Its greater strangeness lies merely in the obviousness of its reversal of the world's thinking. ⁸In the clearest way possible, and at the simplest of levels, the word means the exact opposite to the teachers of God and to the world.

2.   The teacher of God is generous out of Self interest. ²This does not refer, however, to the self of which the world speaks. ³The teacher of God does not want anything he cannot give away, because he realizes it would be valueless to him by definition. ⁴What would he want it *for*? ⁵He could only lose because of it. ⁶He could not gain. ⁷Therefore he does not seek what only he could keep, because that is a guarantee of loss. ⁸He does not want to suffer. ⁹Why should he ensure himself pain? ¹⁰But he does want to keep for himself all things that are of God, and therefore for His Son. ¹¹These are the things that belong to him. ¹²These he can give away in true generosity, protecting them forever for himself.

VIII. Patience

1. Those who are certain of the outcome can afford to wait, and wait without anxiety. [2]Patience is natural to the teacher of God. [3]All he sees is certain outcome, at a time perhaps unknown to him as yet, but not in doubt. [4]The time will be as right as is the answer. [5]And this is true for everything that happens now or in the future. [6]The past as well held no mistakes; nothing that did not serve to benefit the world, as well as him to whom it seemed to happen. [7]Perhaps it was not understood at the time. [8]Even so, the teacher of God is willing to reconsider all his past decisions, if they are causing pain to anyone. [9]Patience is natural to those who trust. [10]Sure of the ultimate interpretation of all things in time, no outcome already seen or yet to come can cause them fear.

IX. Faithfulness

1. The extent of the teacher of God's faithfulness is the measure of his advancement in the curriculum. [2]Does he still select some aspects of his life to bring to his learning, while keeping others apart? [3]If so, his advancement is limited, and his trust not yet firmly established. [4]Faithfulness is the teacher of God's trust in the Word of God to set all things right; not some, but all. [5]Generally, his faithfulness begins by resting on just some problems, remaining carefully limited for a time. [6]To give up all problems to one Answer is to reverse the thinking of the world entirely. [7]And that alone is faithfulness. [8]Nothing but that really deserves the name. [9]Yet each degree, however small, is worth achieving. [10]Readiness, as the text notes, is not mastery.

2. True faithfulness, however, does not deviate. [2]Being consistent, it is wholly honest. [3]Being unswerving, it is full of trust. [4]Being based on fearlessness, it is gentle. [5]Being certain, it is joyous. [6]And being confident, it is tolerant. [7]Faithfulness, then, combines in itself the other attributes of God's teachers. [8]It implies acceptance of the Word of God and His definition of His Son. [9]It is to Them that faithfulness in the true sense is always directed. [10]Toward Them it looks, seeking until it finds. [11]Defenselessness attends it naturally, and joy is its condition. [12]And having found, it rests in quiet certainty on That alone to Which all faithfulness is due.

X. Open-Mindedness

1. The centrality of open-mindedness, perhaps the last of the attributes the teacher of God acquires, is easily understood when its relation to forgiveness is recognized. ²Open-mindedness comes with lack of judgment. ³As judgment shuts the mind against God's Teacher, so open-mindedness invites Him to come in. ⁴As condemnation judges the Son of God as evil, so open-mindedness permits him to be judged by the Voice for God on His behalf. ⁵As the projection of guilt upon him would send him to hell, so open-mindedness lets Christ's image be extended to him. ⁶Only the open-minded can be at peace, for they alone see reason for it.

2. How do the open-minded forgive? ²They have let go all things that would prevent forgiveness. ³They have in truth abandoned the world, and let it be restored to them in newness and in joy so glorious they could never have conceived of such a change. ⁴Nothing is now as it was formerly. ⁵Nothing but sparkles now which seemed so dull and lifeless before. ⁶And above all are all things welcoming, for threat is gone. ⁷No clouds remain to hide the face of Christ. ⁸Now is the goal achieved. ⁹Forgiveness is the final goal of the curriculum. ¹⁰It paves the way for what goes far beyond all learning. ¹¹The curriculum makes no effort to exceed its legitimate goal. ¹²Forgiveness is its single aim, at which all learning ultimately converges. ¹³It is indeed enough.

3. You may have noticed that the list of attributes of God's teachers does not include things that are the Son of God's inheritance. ²Terms like love, sinlessness, perfection, knowledge and eternal truth do not appear in this context. ³They would be most inappropriate here. ⁴What God has given is so far beyond our curriculum that learning but disappears in its presence. ⁵Yet while its presence is obscured, the focus properly belongs on the curriculum. ⁶It is the function of God's teachers to bring true learning to the world. ⁷Properly speaking it is unlearning that they bring, for that is "true learning" in the world. ⁸It is given to the teachers of God to bring the glad tidings of complete forgiveness to the world. ⁹Blessed indeed are they, for they are the bringers of salvation.

5. HOW IS HEALING ACCOMPLISHED?

1.   Healing involves an understanding of what the illusion of sickness is for. ²Healing is impossible without this.

I. The Perceived Purpose of Sickness

1.   Healing is accomplished the instant the sufferer no longer sees any value in pain. ²Who would choose suffering unless he thought it brought him something, and something of value to him? ³He must think it is a small price to pay for something of greater worth. ⁴For sickness is an election; a decision. ⁵It is the choice of weakness, in the mistaken conviction that it is strength. ⁶When this occurs, real strength is seen as threat and health as danger. ⁷Sickness is a method, conceived in madness, for placing God's Son on his Father's throne. ⁸God is seen as outside, fierce and powerful, eager to keep all power for Himself. ⁹Only by His death can He be conquered by His Son.

2.   And what, in this insane conviction, does healing stand for? ²It symbolizes the defeat of God's Son and the triumph of his Father over him. ³It represents the ultimate defiance in a direct form which the Son of God is forced to recognize. ⁴It stands for all that he would hide from himself to protect his "life." ⁵If he is healed, he is responsible for his thoughts. ⁶And if he is responsible for his thoughts, he will be killed to prove to him how weak and pitiful he is. ⁷But if he chooses death himself, his weakness is his strength. ⁸Now has he given himself what God would give to him, and thus entirely usurped the throne of his Creator.

II. The Shift in Perception

1.   Healing must occur in exact proportion to which the valuelessness of sickness is recognized. ²One need but say, "There is no gain at all to me in this" and he is healed. ³But to say this, one first must recognize certain facts. ⁴First, it is obvious that decisions are of the mind, not of the body. ⁵If sickness is but a faulty problem-solving approach, it is a decision. ⁶And if it is a decision, it is the mind and not the body that makes it. ⁷The resistance to recognizing this is enormous, because the existence of the world as you perceive it depends on the body being the

decision maker. [8]Terms like "instincts," "reflexes" and the like represent attempts to endow the body with non-mental motivators. [9]Actually, such terms merely state or describe the problem. [10]They do not answer it.

2. The acceptance of sickness as a decision of the mind, for a purpose for which it would use the body, is the basis of healing. [2]And this is so for healing in all forms. [3]A patient decides that this is so, and he recovers. [4]If he decides against recovery, he will not be healed. [5]Who is the physician? [6]Only the mind of the patient himself. [7]The outcome is what he decides that it is. [8]Special agents seem to be ministering to him, yet they but give form to his own choice. [9]He chooses them in order to bring tangible form to his desires. [10]And it is this they do, and nothing else. [11]They are not actually needed at all. [12]The patient could merely rise up without their aid and say, "I have no use for this." [13]There is no form of sickness that would not be cured at once.

3. What is the single requisite for this shift in perception? [2]It is simply this; the recognition that sickness is of the mind, and has nothing to do with the body. [3]What does this recognition "cost"? [4]It costs the whole world you see, for the world will never again appear to rule the mind. [5]For with this recognition is responsibility placed where it belongs; not with the world, but on him who looks on the world and sees it as it is not. [6]He looks on what he chooses to see. [7]No more and no less. [8]The world does nothing to him. [9]He only thought it did. [10]Nor does he do anything to the world, because he was mistaken about what it is. [11]Herein is the release from guilt and sickness both, for they are one. [12]Yet to accept this release, the insignificance of the body must be an acceptable idea.

4. With this idea is pain forever gone. [2]But with this idea goes also all confusion about creation. [3]Does not this follow of necessity? [4]Place cause and effect in their true sequence in one respect, and the learning will generalize and transform the world. [5]The transfer value of one true idea has no end or limit. [6]The final outcome of this lesson is the remembrance of God. [7]What do guilt and sickness, pain, disaster and all suffering mean now? [8]Having no purpose, they are gone. [9]And with them also go all the effects they seemed to cause. [10]Cause and effect but replicate creation. [11]Seen in their proper perspective, without distortion and without fear, they re-establish Heaven.

III. The Function of the Teacher of God

1. If the patient must change his mind in order to be healed, what does the teacher of God do? ²Can he change the patient's mind for him? ³Certainly not. ⁴For those already willing to change their minds he has no function except to rejoice with them, for they have become teachers of God with him. ⁵He has, however, a more specific function for those who do not understand what healing is. ⁶These patients do not realize they have chosen sickness. ⁷On the contrary, they believe that sickness has chosen them. ⁸Nor are they open-minded on this point. ⁹The body tells them what to do and they obey. ¹⁰They have no idea how insane this concept is. ¹¹If they even suspected it, they would be healed. ¹²Yet they suspect nothing. ¹³To them the separation is quite real.

2. To them God's teachers come, to represent another choice which they had forgotten. ²The simple presence of a teacher of God is a reminder. ³His thoughts ask for the right to question what the patient has accepted as true. ⁴As God's messengers, His teachers are the symbols of salvation. ⁵They ask the patient for forgiveness for God's Son in his own Name. ⁶They stand for the Alternative. ⁷With God's Word in their minds they come in benediction, not to heal the sick but to remind them of the remedy God has already given them. ⁸It is not their hands that heal. ⁹It is not their voice that speaks the Word of God. ¹⁰They merely give what has been given them. ¹¹Very gently they call to their brothers to turn away from death: "Behold, you Son of God, what Life can offer you. ¹²Would you choose sickness in place of this?"

3. Not once do the advanced teachers of God consider the forms of sickness in which their brother believes. ²To do this is to forget that all of them have the same purpose, and therefore are not really different. ³They seek for God's Voice in this brother who would so deceive himself as to believe God's Son can suffer. ⁴And they remind him that he did not make himself, and must remain as God created him. ⁵They recognize illusions can have no effect. ⁶The truth in their minds reaches out to the truth in the minds of their brothers, so that illusions are not reinforced. ⁷They are thus brought to truth; truth is not brought to them. ⁸So are they dispelled, not by the will of another, but by the union of the One Will with Itself. ⁹And this is the function of God's teachers; to see no will as separate from their own, nor theirs as separate from God's.

6. IS HEALING CERTAIN?

1.   Healing is always certain. ²It is impossible to let illusions be brought to truth and keep the illusions. ³Truth demonstrates illusions have no value. ⁴The teacher of God has seen the correction of his errors in the mind of the patient, recognizing it for what it is. ⁵Having accepted the Atonement for himself, he has also accepted it for the patient. ⁶Yet what if the patient uses sickness as a way of life, believing healing is the way to death? ⁷When this is so, a sudden healing might precipitate intense depression, and a sense of loss so deep that the patient might even try to destroy himself. ⁸Having nothing to live for, he may ask for death. ⁹Healing must wait, for his protection.

2.   Healing will always stand aside when it would be seen as threat. ²The instant it is welcome it is there. ³Where healing has been given it will be received. ⁴And what is time before the gifts of God? ⁵We have referred many times in the text to the storehouse of treasures laid up equally for the giver and the receiver of God's gifts. ⁶Not one is lost, for they can but increase. ⁷No teacher of God should feel disappointed if he has offered healing and it does not appear to have been received. ⁸It is not up to him to judge when his gift should be accepted. ⁹Let him be certain it has been received, and trust that it will be accepted when it is recognized as a blessing and not a curse.

3.   It is not the function of God's teachers to evaluate the outcome of their gifts. ²It is merely their function to give them. ³Once they have done that they have also given the outcome, for that is part of the gift. ⁴No one can give if he is concerned with the result of giving. ⁵That is a limitation on the giving itself, and neither the giver nor the receiver would have the gift. ⁶Trust is an essential part of giving; in fact, it is the part that makes sharing possible, the part that guarantees the giver will not lose, but only gain. ⁷Who gives a gift and then remains with it, to be sure it is used as the giver deems appropriate? ⁸Such is not giving but imprisoning.

4.   It is the relinquishing of all concern about the gift that makes it truly given. ²And it is trust that makes true giving possible. ³Healing is the change of mind that the Holy Spirit in the patient's mind is seeking for him. ⁴And it is the Holy Spirit in the mind of the giver Who gives the gift to him. ⁵How can it be lost? ⁶How can it be ineffectual? ⁷How can it be wasted? ⁸God's

treasure house can never be empty. [9]And if one gift is missing, it would not be full. [10]Yet is its fullness guaranteed by God. [11]What concern, then, can a teacher of God have about what becomes of his gifts? [12]Given by God to God, who in this holy exchange can receive less than everything?

7. SHOULD HEALING BE REPEATED?

1.   This question really answers itself. ²Healing cannot be repeated. ³If the patient is healed, what remains to heal him from? ⁴And if the healing is certain, as we have already said it is, what is there to repeat? ⁵For a teacher of God to remain concerned about the result of healing is to limit the healing. ⁶It is now the teacher of God himself whose mind needs to be healed. ⁷And it is this he must facilitate. ⁸He is now the patient, and he must so regard himself. ⁹He has made a mistake, and must be willing to change his mind about it. ¹⁰He lacked the trust that makes for giving truly, and so he has not received the benefit of his gift.

2.   Whenever a teacher of God has tried to be a channel for healing he has succeeded. ²Should he be tempted to doubt this, he should not repeat his previous effort. ³That was already maximal, because the Holy Spirit so accepted it and so used it. ⁴Now the teacher of God has only one course to follow. ⁵He must use his reason to tell himself that he has given the problem to One Who cannot fail, and must recognize that his own uncertainty is not love but fear, and therefore hate. ⁶His position has thus become untenable, for he is offering hate to one to whom he offered love. ⁷This is impossible. ⁸Having offered love, only love can be received.

3.   It is in this that the teacher of God must trust. ²This is what is really meant by the statement that the one responsibility of the miracle worker is to accept the Atonement for himself. ³The teacher of God is a miracle worker because he gives the gifts he has received. ⁴Yet he must first accept them. ⁵He need do no more, nor is there more that he could do. ⁶By accepting healing he can give it. ⁷If he doubts this, let him remember Who gave the gift and Who received it. ⁸Thus is his doubt corrected. ⁹He thought the gifts of God could be withdrawn. ¹⁰That was a mistake, but hardly one to stay with. ¹¹And so the teacher of God can only recognize it for what it is, and let it be corrected for him.

4.   One of the most difficult temptations to recognize is that to doubt a healing because of the appearance of continuing symptoms is a mistake in the form of lack of trust. ²As such it is an attack. ³Usually it seems to be just the opposite. ⁴It does appear unreasonable at first to be told that continued concern is attack. ⁵It has all the appearances of love. ⁶Yet love without trust is impossible, and doubt and trust cannot coexist. ⁷And hate must

22

be the opposite of love, regardless of the form it takes. ⁸Doubt not the gift and it is impossible to doubt its result. ⁹This is the certainty that gives God's teachers the power to be miracle workers, for they have put their trust in Him.

5. The real basis for doubt about the outcome of any problem that has been given to God's Teacher for resolution is always self-doubt. ²And that necessarily implies that trust has been placed in an illusory self, for only such a self can be doubted. ³This illusion can take many forms. ⁴Perhaps there is a fear of weakness and vulnerability. ⁵Perhaps there is a fear of failure and shame associated with a sense of inadequacy. ⁶Perhaps there is a guilty embarrassment stemming from false humility. ⁷The form of the mistake is not important. ⁸What is important is only the recognition of a mistake as a mistake.

6. The mistake is always some form of concern with the self to the exclusion of the patient. ²It is a failure to recognize him as part of the Self, and thus represents a confusion in identity. ³Conflict about what you are has entered your mind, and you have become deceived about yourself. ⁴And you are deceived about yourself because you have denied the Source of your creation. ⁵If you are offering only healing, you cannot doubt. ⁶If you really want the problem solved, you cannot doubt. ⁷If you are certain what the problem is, you cannot doubt. ⁸Doubt is the result of conflicting wishes. ⁹Be sure of what you want, and doubt becomes impossible.

8. HOW CAN PERCEPTION OF ORDER OF DIFFICULTIES
BE AVOIDED?

1. The belief in order of difficulties is the basis for the world's perception. ²It rests on differences; on uneven background and shifting foreground, on unequal heights and diverse sizes, on varying degrees of darkness and light, and thousands of contrasts in which each thing seen competes with every other in order to be recognized. ³A larger object overshadows a smaller one. ⁴A brighter thing draws the attention from another with less intensity of appeal. ⁵And a more threatening idea, or one conceived of as more desirable by the world's standards, completely upsets the mental balance. ⁶What the body's eyes behold is only conflict. ⁷Look not to them for peace and understanding.

2. Illusions are always illusions of differences. ²How could it be otherwise? ³By definition, an illusion is an attempt to make something real that is regarded as of major importance, but is recognized as being untrue. ⁴The mind therefore seeks to make it true out of its intensity of desire to have it for itself. ⁵Illusions are travesties of creation; attempts to bring truth to lies. ⁶Finding truth unacceptable, the mind revolts against truth and gives itself an illusion of victory. ⁷Finding health a burden, it retreats into feverish dreams. ⁸And in these dreams the mind is separate, different from other minds, with different interests of its own, and able to gratify its needs at the expense of others.

3. Where do all these differences come from? ²Certainly they seem to be in the world outside. ³Yet it is surely the mind that judges what the eyes behold. ⁴It is the mind that interprets the eyes' messages and gives them "meaning." ⁵And this meaning does not exist in the world outside at all. ⁶What is seen as "reality" is simply what the mind prefers. ⁷Its hierarchy of values is projected outward, and it sends the body's eyes to find it. ⁸The body's eyes will never see except through differences. ⁹Yet it is not the messages they bring on which perception rests. ¹⁰Only the mind evaluates their messages, and so only the mind is responsible for seeing. ¹¹It alone decides whether what is seen is real or illusory, desirable or undesirable, pleasurable or painful.

4. It is in the sorting out and categorizing activities of the mind that errors in perception enter. ²And it is here correction must be made. ³The mind classifies what the body's eyes bring to it according to its preconceived values, judging where each sense

datum fits best. [4]What basis could be faultier than this? [5]Unrecognized by itself, it has itself asked to be given what will fit into these categories. [6]And having done so, it concludes that the categories must be true. [7]On this the judgment of all differences rests, because it is on this that judgments of the world depend. [8]Can this confused and senseless "reasoning" be depended on for anything?

5. There can be no order of difficulty in healing merely because all sickness is illusion. [2]Is it harder to dispel the belief of the insane in a larger hallucination as opposed to a smaller one? [3]Will he agree more quickly to the unreality of a louder voice he hears than to that of a softer one? [4]Will he dismiss more easily a whispered demand to kill than a shout? [5]And do the number of pitchforks the devils he sees carrying affect their credibility in his perception? [6]His mind has categorized them all as real, and so they are all real to him. [7]When he realizes they are all illusions they will disappear. [8]And so it is with healing. [9]The properties of illusions which seem to make them different are really irrelevant, for their properties are as illusory as they are.

6. The body's eyes will continue to see differences. [2]But the mind that has let itself be healed will no longer acknowledge them. [3]There will be those who seem to be "sicker" than others, and the body's eyes will report their changed appearances as before. [4]But the healed mind will put them all in one category; they are unreal. [5]This is the gift of its Teacher; the understanding that only two categories are meaningful in sorting out the messages the mind receives from what appears to be the outside world. [6]And of these two, but one is real. [7]Just as reality is wholly real, apart from size and shape and time and place—for differences cannot exist within it—so too are illusions without distinctions. [8]The one answer to sickness of any kind is healing. [9]The one answer to all illusions is truth.

9. ARE CHANGES REQUIRED IN THE LIFE SITUATION OF GOD'S TEACHERS?

1.   Changes are required in the *minds* of God's teachers. ²This may or may not involve changes in the external situation. ³Remember that no one is where he is by accident, and chance plays no part in God's plan. ⁴It is most unlikely that changes in attitudes would not be the first step in the newly-made teacher of God's training. ⁵There is, however, no set pattern, since training is always highly individualized. ⁶There are those who are called upon to change their life situation almost immediately, but these are generally special cases. ⁷By far the majority are given a slowly-evolving training program, in which as many previous mistakes as possible are corrected. ⁸Relationships in particular must be properly perceived, and all dark cornerstones of unforgiveness removed. ⁹Otherwise the old thought system still has a basis for return.

2.   As the teacher of God advances in his training, he learns one lesson with increasing thoroughness. ²He does not make his own decisions; he asks his Teacher for His answer, and it is this he follows as his guide for action. ³This becomes easier and easier, as the teacher of God learns to give up his own judgment. ⁴The giving up of judgment, the obvious prerequisite for hearing God's Voice, is usually a fairly slow process, not because it is difficult, but because it is apt to be perceived as personally insulting. ⁵The world's training is directed toward achieving a goal in direct opposition to that of our curriculum. ⁶The world trains for reliance on one's judgment as the criterion for maturity and strength. ⁷Our curriculum trains for the relinquishment of judgment as the necessary condition of salvation.

10. HOW IS JUDGMENT RELINQUISHED?

1. Judgment, like other devices by which the world of illusions is maintained, is totally misunderstood by the world. ²It is actually confused with wisdom, and substitutes for truth. ³As the world uses the term, an individual is capable of "good" and "bad" judgment, and his education aims at strengthening the former and minimizing the latter. ⁴There is, however, considerable confusion about what these categories mean. ⁵What is "good" judgment to one is "bad" judgment to another. ⁶Further, even the same person classifies the same action as showing "good" judgment at one time and "bad" judgment at another time. ⁷Nor can any consistent criteria for determining what these categories are be really taught. ⁸At any time the student may disagree with what his would-be teacher says about them, and the teacher himself may well be inconsistent in what he believes. ⁹"Good" judgment, in these terms, does not mean anything. ¹⁰No more does "bad."

2. It is necessary for the teacher of God to realize, not that he should not judge, but that he cannot. ²In giving up judgment, he is merely giving up what he did not have. ³He gives up an illusion; or better, he has an illusion of giving up. ⁴He has actually merely become more honest. ⁵Recognizing that judgment was always impossible for him, he no longer attempts it. ⁶This is no sacrifice. ⁷On the contrary, he puts himself in a position where judgment *through* him rather than *by* him can occur. ⁸And this judgment is neither "good" nor "bad." ⁹It is the only judgment there is, and it is only one: "God's Son is guiltless, and sin does not exist."

3. The aim of our curriculum, unlike the goal of the world's learning, is the recognition that judgment in the usual sense is impossible. ²This is not an opinion but a fact. ³In order to judge anything rightly, one would have to be fully aware of an inconceivably wide range of things; past, present and to come. ⁴One would have to recognize in advance all the effects of his judgments on everyone and everything involved in them in any way. ⁵And one would have to be certain there is no distortion in his perception, so that his judgment would be wholly fair to everyone on whom it rests now and in the future. ⁶Who is in a position to do this? ⁷Who except in grandiose fantasies would claim this for himself?

4. Remember how many times you thought you knew all the "facts" you needed for judgment, and how wrong you were! ²Is there anyone who has not had this experience? ³Would you know how many times you merely thought you were right, without ever realizing you were wrong? ⁴Why would you choose such an arbitrary basis for decision making? ⁵Wisdom is not judgment; it is the relinquishment of judgment. ⁶Make then but one more judgment. ⁷It is this: There is Someone with you Whose judgment is perfect. ⁸He does know all the facts; past, present and to come. ⁹He does know all the effects of His judgment on everyone and everything involved in any way. ¹⁰And He is wholly fair to everyone, for there is no distortion in His perception.

5. Therefore lay judgment down, not with regret but with a sigh of gratitude. ²Now are you free of a burden so great that you could merely stagger and fall down beneath it. ³And it was all illusion. ⁴Nothing more. ⁵Now can the teacher of God rise up unburdened, and walk lightly on. ⁶Yet it is not only this that is his benefit. ⁷His sense of care is gone, for he has none. ⁸He has given it away, along with judgment. ⁹He gave himself to Him Whose judgment he has chosen now to trust, instead of his own. ¹⁰Now he makes no mistakes. ¹¹His Guide is sure. ¹²And where he came to judge, he comes to bless. ¹³Where now he laughs, he used to come to weep.

6. It is not difficult to relinquish judgment. ²But it is difficult indeed to try to keep it. ³The teacher of God lays it down happily the instant he recognizes its cost. ⁴All of the ugliness he sees about him is its outcome. ⁵All of the pain he looks upon is its result. ⁶All of the loneliness and sense of loss; of passing time and growing hopelessness; of sickening despair and fear of death; all these have come of it. ⁷And now he knows that these things need not be. ⁸Not one is true. ⁹For he has given up their cause, and they, which never were but the effects of his mistaken choice, have fallen from him. ¹⁰Teacher of God, this step will bring you peace. ¹¹Can it be difficult to want but this?

11. HOW IS PEACE POSSIBLE IN THIS WORLD?

1. This is a question everyone must ask. ²Certainly peace seems to be impossible here. ³Yet the Word of God promises other things that seem impossible, as well as this. ⁴His Word has promised peace. ⁵It has also promised that there is no death, that resurrection must occur, and that rebirth is man's inheritance. ⁶The world you see cannot be the world God loves, and yet His Word assures us that He loves the world. ⁷God's Word has promised that peace is possible here, and what He promises can hardly be impossible. ⁸But it is true that the world must be looked at differently, if His promises are to be accepted. ⁹What the world is, is but a fact. ¹⁰You cannot choose what this should be. ¹¹But you can choose how you would see it. ¹²Indeed, you *must* choose this.

2. Again we come to the question of judgment. ²This time ask yourself whether your judgment or the Word of God is more likely to be true. ³For they say different things about the world, and things so opposite that it is pointless to try to reconcile them. ⁴God offers the world salvation; your judgment would condemn it. ⁵God says there is no death; your judgment sees but death as the inevitable end of life. ⁶God's Word assures you that He loves the world; your judgment says it is unlovable. ⁷Who is right? ⁸For one of you is wrong. ⁹It must be so.

3. The text explains that the Holy Spirit is the Answer to all problems you have made. ²These problems are not real, but that is meaningless to those who believe in them. ³And everyone believes in what he made, for it was made by his believing it. ⁴Into this strange and paradoxical situation,—one without meaning and devoid of sense, yet out of which no way seems possible,—God has sent His Judgment to answer yours. ⁵Gently His Judgment substitutes for yours. ⁶And through this substitution is the un-understandable made understandable. ⁷How is peace possible in this world? ⁸In your judgment it is not possible, and can never be possible. ⁹But in the Judgment of God what is reflected here is only peace.

4. Peace is impossible to those who look on war. ²Peace is inevitable to those who offer peace. ³How easily, then, is your judgment of the world escaped! ⁴It is not the world that makes peace seem impossible. ⁵It is the world you see that is impossible. ⁶Yet

has God's Judgment on this distorted world redeemed it and made it fit to welcome peace. [7]And peace descends on it in joyous answer. [8]Peace now belongs here, because a Thought of God has entered. [9]What else but a Thought of God turns hell to Heaven merely by being what it is? [10]The earth bows down before its gracious Presence, and it leans down in answer, to raise it up again. [11]Now is the question different. [12]It is no longer, "Can peace be possible in this world?" but instead, "Is it not impossible that peace be absent here?"

12. HOW MANY TEACHERS OF GOD ARE NEEDED TO SAVE THE WORLD?

1.   The answer to this question is—one. ²One wholly perfect teacher, whose learning is complete, suffices. ³This one, sanctified and redeemed, becomes the Self Who is the Son of God. ⁴He who was always wholly spirit now no longer sees himself as a body, or even as in a body. ⁵Therefore he is limitless. ⁶And being limitless, his thoughts are joined with God's forever and ever. ⁷His perception of himself is based upon God's Judgment, not his own. ⁸Thus does he share God's Will, and bring His thoughts to still deluded minds. ⁹He is forever one, because he is as God created him. ¹⁰He has accepted Christ, and he is saved.

2.   Thus does the son of man become the Son of God. ²It is not really a change; it is a change of mind. ³Nothing external alters, but everything internal now reflects only the Love of God. ⁴God can no longer be feared, for the mind sees no cause for punishment. ⁵God's teachers appear to be many, for that is what is the world's need. ⁶Yet being joined in one purpose, and one they share with God, how could they be separate from each other? ⁷What does it matter if they then appear in many forms? ⁸Their minds are one; their joining is complete. ⁹And God works through them now as one, for that is what they are.

3.   Why is the illusion of many necessary? ²Only because reality is not understandable to the deluded. ³Only very few can hear God's Voice at all, and even they cannot communicate His messages directly through the Spirit Which gave them. ⁴They need a medium through which communication becomes possible to those who do not realize that they are spirit. ⁵A body they can see. ⁶A voice they understand and listen to, without the fear that truth would encounter in them. ⁷Do not forget that truth can come only where it is welcomed without fear. ⁸So do God's teachers need a body, for their unity could not be recognized directly.

4.   Yet what makes God's teachers is their recognition of the proper purpose of the body. ²As they advance in their profession, they become more and more certain that the body's function is but to let God's Voice speak through it to human ears. ³And these ears will carry to the mind of the hearer messages that are not of this world, and the mind will understand because of their Source. ⁴From this understanding will come the recognition, in this new teacher of God, of what the body's purpose really is; the only use

there really is for it. ⁵This lesson is enough to let the thought of unity come in, and what is one is recognized as one. ⁶The teachers of God appear to share the illusion of separation, but because of what they use the body for, they do not believe in the illusion despite appearances.

5. The central lesson is always this; that what you use the body for it will become to you. ²Use it for sin or for attack, which is the same as sin, and you will see it as sinful. ³Because it is sinful it is weak, and being weak, it suffers and it dies. ⁴Use it to bring the Word of God to those who have it not, and the body becomes holy. ⁵Because it is holy it cannot be sick, nor can it die. ⁶When its usefulness is done it is laid by, and that is all. ⁷The mind makes this decision, as it makes all decisions that are responsible for the body's condition. ⁸Yet the teacher of God does not make this decision alone. ⁹To do that would be to give the body another purpose from the one that keeps it holy. ¹⁰God's Voice will tell him when he has fulfilled his role, just as It tells him what his function is. ¹¹He does not suffer either in going or remaining. ¹²Sickness is now impossible to him.

6. Oneness and sickness cannot coexist. ²God's teachers choose to look on dreams a while. ³It is a conscious choice. ⁴For they have learned that all choices are made consciously, with full awareness of their consequences. ⁵The dream says otherwise, but who would put his faith in dreams once they are recognized for what they are? ⁶Awareness of dreaming is the real function of God's teachers. ⁷They watch the dream figures come and go, shift and change, suffer and die. ⁸Yet they are not deceived by what they see. ⁹They recognize that to behold a dream figure as sick and separate is no more real than to regard it as healthy and beautiful. ¹⁰Unity alone is not a thing of dreams. ¹¹And it is this God's teachers acknowledge as behind the dream, beyond all seeming and yet surely theirs.

13. WHAT IS THE REAL MEANING OF SACRIFICE?

1.   Although in truth the term sacrifice is altogether meaningless, it does have meaning in the world. ²Like all things in the world, its meaning is temporary and will ultimately fade into the nothingness from which it came when there is no more use for it. ³Now its real meaning is a lesson. ⁴Like all lessons it is an illusion, for in reality there is nothing to learn. ⁵Yet this illusion must be replaced by a corrective device; another illusion that replaces the first, so both can finally disappear. ⁶The first illusion, which must be displaced before another thought system can take hold, is that it is a sacrifice to give up the things of this world. ⁷What could this be but an illusion, since this world itself is nothing more than that?

2.   It takes great learning both to realize and to accept the fact that the world has nothing to give. ²What can the sacrifice of nothing mean? ³It cannot mean that you have less because of it. ⁴There is no sacrifice in the world's terms that does not involve the body. ⁵Think a while about what the world calls sacrifice. ⁶Power, fame, money, physical pleasure; who is the "hero" to whom all these things belong? ⁷Could they mean anything except to a body? ⁸Yet a body cannot evaluate. ⁹By seeking after such things the mind associates itself with the body, obscuring its identity and losing sight of what it really is.

3.   Once this confusion has occurred, it becomes impossible for the mind to understand that all the "pleasures" of the world are nothing. ²But what a sacrifice,—and it is sacrifice indeed! — all this entails. ³Now has the mind condemned itself to seek without finding; to be forever dissatisfied and discontented; to know not what it really wants to find. ⁴Who can escape this self-condemnation? ⁵Only through God's Word could this be possible. ⁶For self-condemnation is a decision about identity, and no one doubts what he believes he is. ⁷He can doubt all things, but never this.

4.   God's teachers can have no regret on giving up the pleasures of the world. ²Is it a sacrifice to give up pain? ³Does an adult resent the giving up of children's toys? ⁴Does one whose vision has already glimpsed the face of Christ look back with longing on a slaughter house? ⁵No one who has escaped the world and all its ills looks back on it with condemnation. ⁶Yet he must rejoice that he is free of all the sacrifice its values would demand of him. ⁷To

them he sacrifices all his peace. [8]To them he sacrifices all his freedom. [9]And to possess them must he sacrifice his hope of Heaven and remembrance of his Father's Love. [10]Who in his sane mind chooses nothing as a substitute for everything?

5. What is the real meaning of sacrifice? [2]It is the cost of believing in illusions. [3]It is the price that must be paid for the denial of truth. [4]There is no pleasure of the world that does not demand this, for otherwise the pleasure would be seen as pain, and no one asks for pain if he recognizes it. [5]It is the idea of sacrifice that makes him blind. [6]He does not see what he is asking for. [7]And so he seeks it in a thousand ways and in a thousand places, each time believing it is there, and each time disappointed in the end. [8]"Seek but do not find" remains this world's stern decree, and no one who pursues the world's goals can do otherwise.

6. You may believe this course requires sacrifice of all you really hold dear. [2]In one sense this is true, for you hold dear the things that crucify God's Son, and it is the course's aim to set him free. [3]But do not be mistaken about what sacrifice means. [4]It always means the giving up of what you want. [5]And what, O teacher of God, is it that you want? [6]You have been called by God, and you have answered. [7]Would you now sacrifice that Call? [8]Few have heard it as yet, and they can but turn to you. [9]There is no other hope in all the world that they can trust. [10]There is no other voice in all the world that echoes God's. [11]If you would sacrifice the truth, they stay in hell. [12]And if they stay, you will remain with them.

7. Do not forget that sacrifice is total. [2]There are no half sacrifices. [3]You cannot give up Heaven partially. [4]You cannot be a little bit in hell. [5]The Word of God has no exceptions. [6]It is this that makes it holy and beyond the world. [7]It is its holiness that points to God. [8]It is its holiness that makes you safe. [9]It is denied if you attack any brother for anything. [10]For it is here the split with God occurs. [11]A split that is impossible. [12]A split that cannot happen. [13]Yet a split in which you surely will believe, because you have set up a situation that is impossible. [14]And in this situation the impossible can seem to happen. [15]It seems to happen at the "sacrifice" of truth.

8. Teacher of God, do not forget the meaning of sacrifice, and remember what each decision you make must mean in terms of cost. [2]Decide for God, and everything is given you at no cost at all. [3]Decide against Him, and you choose nothing, at the expense

of the awareness of everything. ⁴What would you teach? ⁵Remember only what you would learn. ⁶For it is here that your concern should be. ⁷Atonement is for you. ⁸Your learning claims it and your learning gives it. ⁹The world contains it not. ¹⁰But learn this course and it is yours. ¹¹God holds out His Word to you, for He has need of teachers. ¹²What other way is there to save His Son?

14. HOW WILL THE WORLD END?

1. Can what has no beginning really end? ²The world will end in an illusion, as it began. ³Yet will its ending be an illusion of mercy. ⁴The illusion of forgiveness, complete, excluding no one, limitless in gentleness, will cover it, hiding all evil, concealing all sin and ending guilt forever. ⁵So ends the world that guilt had made, for now it has no purpose and is gone. ⁶The father of illusions is the belief that they have a purpose; that they serve a need or gratify a want. ⁷Perceived as purposeless, they are no longer seen. ⁸Their uselessness is recognized, and they are gone. ⁹How but in this way are all illusions ended? ¹⁰They have been brought to truth, and truth saw them not. ¹¹It merely overlooked the meaningless.

2. Until forgiveness is complete, the world does have a purpose. ²It becomes the home in which forgiveness is born, and where it grows and becomes stronger and more all-embracing. ³Here is it nourished, for here it is needed. ⁴A gentle Savior, born where sin was made and guilt seemed real. ⁵Here is His home, for here there is need of Him indeed. ⁶He brings the ending of the world with Him. ⁷It is His Call God's teachers answer, turning to Him in silence to receive His Word. ⁸The world will end when all things in it have been rightly judged by His judgment. ⁹The world will end with the benediction of holiness upon it. ¹⁰When not one thought of sin remains, the world is over. ¹¹It will not be destroyed nor attacked nor even touched. ¹²It will merely cease to seem to be.

3. Certainly this seems to be a long, long while away. ²"When not one thought of sin remains" appears to be a long-range goal indeed. ³But time stands still, and waits on the goal of God's teachers. ⁴Not one thought of sin will remain the instant any one of them accepts Atonement for himself. ⁵It is not easier to forgive one sin than to forgive all of them. ⁶The illusion of orders of difficulty is an obstacle the teacher of God must learn to pass by and leave behind. ⁷One sin perfectly forgiven by one teacher of God can make salvation complete. ⁸Can you understand this? ⁹No; it is meaningless to anyone here. ¹⁰Yet it is the final lesson in which unity is restored. ¹¹It goes against all the thinking of the world, but so does Heaven.

4. The world will end when its thought system has been com-

pletely reversed. ²Until then, bits and pieces of its thinking will still seem sensible. ³The final lesson, which brings the ending of the world, cannot be grasped by those not yet prepared to leave the world and go beyond its tiny reach. ⁴What, then, is the function of the teacher of God in this concluding lesson? ⁵He need merely learn how to approach it; to be willing to go in its direction. ⁶He need merely trust that, if God's Voice tells him it is a lesson he can learn, he can learn it. ⁷He does not judge it either as hard or easy. ⁸His Teacher points to it, and he trusts that He will show him how to learn it.

5. The world will end in joy, because it is a place of sorrow. ²When joy has come, the purpose of the world has gone. ³The world will end in peace, because it is a place of war. ⁴When peace has come, what is the purpose of the world? ⁵The world will end in laughter, because it is a place of tears. ⁶Where there is laughter, who can longer weep? ⁷And only complete forgiveness brings all this to bless the world. ⁸In blessing it departs, for it will not end as it began. ⁹To turn hell into Heaven is the function of God's teachers, for what they teach are lessons in which Heaven is reflected. ¹⁰And now sit down in true humility, and realize that all God would have you do you can do. ¹¹Do not be arrogant and say you cannot learn His Own curriculum. ¹²His Word says otherwise. ¹³His Will be done. ¹⁴It cannot be otherwise. ¹⁵And be you thankful it is so.

15. IS EACH ONE TO BE JUDGED IN THE END?

1.   Indeed, yes! [2]No one can escape God's Final Judgment. [3]Who could flee forever from the truth? [4]But the Final Judgment will not come until it is no longer associated with fear. [5]One day each one will welcome it, and on that very day it will be given him. [6]He will hear his sinlessness proclaimed around and around the world, setting it free as God's Final Judgment on him is received. [7]This is the Judgment in which salvation lies. [8]This is the Judgment that will set him free. [9]This is the Judgment in which all things are freed with him. [10]Time pauses as eternity comes near, and silence lies across the world that everyone may hear this Judgment of the Son of God:

> [11]*Holy are you, eternal, free and whole, at peace forever in the Heart of God.* [12]*Where is the world, and where is sorrow now?*

2.   Is this your judgment on yourself, teacher of God? [2]Do you believe that this is wholly true? [3]No; not yet, not yet. [4]But this is still your goal; why you are here. [5]It is your function to prepare yourself to hear this Judgment and to recognize that it is true. [6]One instant of complete belief in this, and you will go beyond belief to Certainty. [7]One instant out of time can bring time's end. [8]Judge not, for you but judge yourself, and thus delay this Final Judgment. [9]What is your judgment of the world, teacher of God? [10]Have you yet learned to stand aside and hear the Voice of Judgment in yourself? [11]Or do you still attempt to take His role from Him? [12]Learn to be quiet, for His Voice is heard in stillness. [13]And His Judgment comes to all who stand aside in quiet listening, and wait for Him.

3.   You who are sometimes sad and sometimes angry; who sometimes feel your just due is not given you, and your best efforts meet with lack of appreciation and even contempt; give up these foolish thoughts! [2]They are too small and meaningless to occupy your holy mind an instant longer. [3]God's Judgment waits for you to set you free. [4]What can the world hold out to you, regardless of your judgments on its gifts, that you would rather have? [5]You will be judged, and judged in fairness and in honesty. [6]There is no deceit in God. [7]His promises are sure. [8]Only remember that.

⁹His promises have guaranteed His Judgment, and His alone, will be accepted in the end. ¹⁰It is your function to make that end be soon. ¹¹It is your function to hold it to your heart, and offer it to all the world to keep it safe.

16. HOW SHOULD THE TEACHER OF GOD
SPEND HIS DAY?

1. To the advanced teacher of God this question is meaningless. ²There is no program, for the lessons change each day. ³Yet the teacher of God is sure of but one thing; they do not change at random. ⁴Seeing this and understanding that it is true, he rests content. ⁵He will be told all that his role should be, this day and every day. ⁶And those who share that role with him will find him, so they can learn the lessons for the day together. ⁷Not one is absent whom he needs; not one is sent without a learning goal already set, and one which can be learned that very day. ⁸For the advanced teacher of God, then, this question is superfluous. ⁹It has been asked and answered, and he keeps in constant contact with the Answer. ¹⁰He is set, and sees the road on which he walks stretch surely and smoothly before him.

2. But what about those who have not reached his certainty? ²They are not yet ready for such lack of structuring on their own part. ³What must they do to learn to give the day to God? ⁴There are some general rules which do apply, although each one must use them as best he can in his own way. ⁵Routines as such are dangerous, because they easily become gods in their own right, threatening the very goals for which they were set up. ⁶Broadly speaking, then, it can be said that it is well to start the day right. ⁷It is always possible to begin again, should the day begin with error. ⁸Yet there are obvious advantages in terms of saving time.

3. At the beginning, it is wise to think in terms of time. ²This is by no means the ultimate criterion, but at the outset it is probably the simplest to observe. ³The saving of time is an essential early emphasis which, although it remains important throughout the learning process, becomes less and less emphasized. ⁴At the outset, we can safely say that time devoted to starting the day right does indeed save time. ⁵How much time should be so spent? ⁶This must depend on the teacher of God himself. ⁷He cannot claim that title until he has gone through the workbook, since we are learning within the framework of our course. ⁸After completion of the more structured practice periods, which the workbook contains, individual need becomes the chief consideration.

4. This course is always practical. ²It may be that the teacher of God is not in a situation that fosters quiet thought as he awakes. ³If this is so, let him but remember that he chooses to spend time

with God as soon as possible, and let him do so. ⁴Duration is not the major concern. ⁵One can easily sit still an hour with closed eyes and accomplish nothing. ⁶One can as easily give God only an instant, and in that instant join with Him completely. ⁷Perhaps the one generalization that can be made is this; as soon as possible after waking take your quiet time, continuing a minute or two after you begin to find it difficult. ⁸You may find that the difficulty will diminish and drop away. ⁹If not, that is the time to stop.

5. The same procedures should be followed at night. ²Perhaps your quiet time should be fairly early in the evening, if it is not feasible for you to take it just before going to sleep. ³It is not wise to lie down for it. ⁴It is better to sit up, in whatever position you prefer. ⁵Having gone through the workbook, you must have come to some conclusions in this respect. ⁶If possible, however, just before going to sleep is a desirable time to devote to God. ⁷It sets your mind into a pattern of rest, and orients you away from fear. ⁸If it is expedient to spend this time earlier, at least be sure that you do not forget a brief period,—not more than a moment will do,—in which you close your eyes and think of God.

6. There is one thought in particular that should be remembered throughout the day. ²It is a thought of pure joy; a thought of peace, a thought of limitless release, limitless because all things are freed within it. ³You think you made a place of safety for yourself. ⁴You think you made a power that can save you from all the fearful things you see in dreams. ⁵It is not so. ⁶Your safety lies not there. ⁷What you give up is merely the illusion of protecting illusions. ⁸And it is this you fear, and only this. ⁹How foolish to be so afraid of nothing! ¹⁰Nothing at all! ¹¹Your defenses will not work, but you are not in danger. ¹²You have no need of them. ¹³Recognize this, and they will disappear. ¹⁴And only then will you accept your real protection.

7. How simply and how easily does time slip by for the teacher of God who has accepted His protection! ²All that he did before in the name of safety no longer interests him. ³For he is safe, and knows it to be so. ⁴He has a Guide Who will not fail. ⁵He need make no distinctions among the problems he perceives, for He to Whom he turns with all of them recognizes no order of difficulty in resolving them. ⁶He is as safe in the present as he was before illusions were accepted into his mind, and as he will be when he has let them go. ⁷There is no difference in his state at different times and different places, because they are all one to God. ⁸This

41

is his safety. ⁹And he has no need for more than this.

8. Yet there will be temptations along the way the teacher of God has yet to travel, and he has need of reminding himself throughout the day of his protection. ²How can he do this, particularly during the time when his mind is occupied with external things? ³He can but try, and his success depends on his conviction that he will succeed. ⁴He must be sure success is not of him, but will be given him at any time, in any place and circumstance he calls for it. ⁵There are times his certainty will waver, and the instant this occurs he will return to earlier attempts to place reliance on himself alone. ⁶Forget not this is magic, and magic is a sorry substitute for true assistance. ⁷It is not good enough for God's teacher, because it is not enough for God's Son.

9. The avoidance of magic is the avoidance of temptation. ²For all temptation is nothing more than the attempt to substitute another will for God's. ³These attempts may indeed seem frightening, but they are merely pathetic. ⁴They can have no effects; neither good nor bad, neither rewarding nor demanding sacrifice, healing nor destructive, quieting nor fearful. ⁵When all magic is recognized as merely nothing, the teacher of God has reached the most advanced state. ⁶All intermediate lessons will but lead to this, and bring this goal nearer to recognition. ⁷For magic of any kind, in all its forms, simply does nothing. ⁸Its powerlessness is the reason it can be so easily escaped. ⁹What has no effects can hardly terrify.

10. There is no substitute for the Will of God. ²In simple statement, it is to this fact that the teacher of God devotes his day. ³Each substitute he may accept as real can but deceive him. ⁴But he is safe from all deception if he so decides. ⁵Perhaps he needs to remember, "God is with me. ⁶I cannot be deceived." ⁷Perhaps he prefers other words, or only one, or none at all. ⁸Yet each temptation to accept magic as true must be abandoned through his recognition, not that it is fearful, not that it is sinful, not that it is dangerous, but merely that it is meaningless. ⁹Rooted in sacrifice and separation, two aspects of one error and no more, he merely chooses to give up all that he never had. ¹⁰And for this "sacrifice" is Heaven restored to his awareness.

11. Is not this an exchange that you would want? ²The world would gladly make it, if it knew it could be made. ³It is God's teachers who must teach it that it can. ⁴And so it is their function to make sure that they have learned it. ⁵No risk is possible throughout the day except to put your trust in magic, for it is

only this that leads to pain. [6]"There is no will but God's." [7]His teachers know that this is so, and have learned that everything but this is magic. [8]All belief in magic is maintained by just one simple-minded illusion;—that it works. [9]All through his training, every day and every hour, and even every minute and second, must God's teachers learn to recognize the forms of magic and perceive their meaninglessness. [10]Fear is withdrawn from them, and so they go. [11]And thus the gate of Heaven is reopened, and its light can shine again on an untroubled mind.

17. HOW DO GOD'S TEACHERS DEAL WITH
MAGIC THOUGHTS?

1.   This is a crucial question both for teacher and pupil. ²If this issue is mishandled, the teacher of God has hurt himself and has also attacked his pupil. ³This strengthens fear, and makes the magic seem quite real to both of them. ⁴How to deal with magic thus becomes a major lesson for the teacher of God to master. ⁵His first responsibility in this is not to attack it. ⁶If a magic thought arouses anger in any form, God's teacher can be sure that he is strengthening his own belief in sin and has condemned himself. ⁷He can be sure as well that he has asked for depression, pain, fear and disaster to come to him. ⁸Let him remember, then, it is not this that he would teach, because it is not this that he would learn.

2.   There is, however, a temptation to respond to magic in a way that reinforces it. ²Nor is this always obvious. ³It can, in fact, be easily concealed beneath a wish to help. ⁴It is this double wish that makes the help of little value, and must lead to undesired outcomes. ⁵Nor should it be forgotten that the outcome that results will always come to teacher and to pupil alike. ⁶How many times has it been emphasized that you give but to yourself? ⁷And where could this be better shown than in the kinds of help the teacher of God gives to those who need his aid? ⁸Here is his gift most clearly given him. ⁹For he will give only what he has chosen for himself. ¹⁰And in this gift is his judgment upon the holy Son of God.

3.   It is easiest to let error be corrected where it is most apparent, and errors can be recognized by their results. ²A lesson truly taught can lead to nothing but release for teacher and pupil, who have shared in one intent. ³Attack can enter only if perception of separate goals has entered. ⁴And this must indeed have been the case if the result is anything but joy. ⁵The single aim of the teacher turns the divided goal of the pupil into one direction, with the call for help becoming his one appeal. ⁶This then is easily responded to with just one answer, and this answer will enter the teacher's mind unfailingly. ⁷From there it shines into his pupil's mind, making it one with his.

4.   Perhaps it will be helpful to remember that no one can be angry at a fact. ²It is always an interpretation that gives rise to negative emotions, regardless of their seeming justification by

what *appears* as facts. ³Regardless, too, of the intensity of the anger that is aroused. ⁴It may be merely slight irritation, perhaps too mild to be even clearly recognized. ⁵Or it may also take the form of intense rage, accompanied by thoughts of violence, fantasied or apparently acted out. ⁶It does not matter. ⁷All of these reactions are the same. ⁸They obscure the truth, and this can never be a matter of degree. ⁹Either truth is apparent, or it is not. ¹⁰It cannot be partially recognized. ¹¹Who is unaware of truth must look upon illusions.

5. Anger in response to perceived magic thoughts is a basic cause of fear. ²Consider what this reaction means, and its centrality in the world's thought system becomes apparent. ³A magic thought, by its mere presence, acknowledges a separation from God. ⁴It states, in the clearest form possible, that the mind which believes it has a separate will that can oppose the Will of God, also believes it can succeed. ⁵That this can hardly be a fact is obvious. ⁶Yet that it can be believed as fact is equally obvious. ⁷And herein lies the birthplace of guilt. ⁸Who usurps the place of God and takes it for himself now has a deadly "enemy." ⁹And he must stand alone in his protection, and make himself a shield to keep him safe from fury that can never be abated, and vengeance that can never be satisfied.

6. How can this unfair battle be resolved? ²Its ending is inevitable, for its outcome must be death. ³How, then, can one believe in one's defenses? ⁴Magic again must help. ⁵Forget the battle. ⁶Accept it as a fact, and then forget it. ⁷Do not remember the impossible odds against you. ⁸Do not remember the immensity of the "enemy," and do not think about your frailty in comparison. ⁹Accept your separation, but do not remember how it came about. ¹⁰Believe that you have won it, but do not retain the slightest memory of Who your great "opponent" really is. ¹¹Projecting your "forgetting" onto Him, it seems to you He has forgotten, too.

7. But what will now be your reaction to all magic thoughts? ²They can but reawaken sleeping guilt, which you have hidden but have not let go. ³Each one says clearly to your frightened mind, "You have usurped the place of God. ⁴Think not He has forgotten." ⁵Here we have the fear of God most starkly represented. ⁶For in that thought has guilt already raised madness to the throne of God Himself. ⁷And now there is no hope. ⁸Except to kill. ⁹Here is salvation now. ¹⁰An angry father pursues his guilty

son. [11]Kill or be killed, for here alone is choice. [12]Beyond this there is none, for what was done cannot be done without. [13]The stain of blood can never be removed, and anyone who bears this stain on him must meet with death.

8. Into this hopeless situation God sends His teachers. [2]They bring the light of hope from God Himself. [3]There is a way in which escape is possible. [4]It can be learned and taught, but it requires patience and abundant willingness. [5]Given that, the lesson's manifest simplicity stands out like an intense white light against a black horizon, for such it is. [6]If anger comes from an interpretation and not a fact, it is never justified. [7]Once this is even dimly grasped, the way is open. [8]Now it is possible to take the next step. [9]The interpretation can be changed at last. [10]Magic thoughts need not lead to condemnation, for they do not really have the power to give rise to guilt. [11]And so they can be overlooked, and thus forgotten in the truest sense.

9. Madness but seems terrible. [2]In truth it has no power to make anything. [3]Like the magic which becomes its servant, it neither attacks nor protects. [4]To see it and to recognize its thought system is to look on nothing. [5]Can nothing give rise to anger? [6]Hardly so. [7]Remember, then, teacher of God, that anger recognizes a reality that is not there; yet is the anger certain witness that you do believe in it as fact. [8]Now is escape impossible, until you see you have responded to your own interpretation, which you have projected on an outside world. [9]Let this grim sword be taken from you now. [10]There is no death. [11]This sword does not exist. [12]The fear of God is causeless. [13]But His Love is Cause of everything beyond all fear, and thus forever real and always true.

18. HOW IS CORRECTION MADE?

1.   Correction of a lasting nature,—and only this is true correction,—cannot be made until the teacher of God has ceased to confuse interpretation with fact, or illusion with truth. ²If he argues with his pupil about a magic thought, attacks it, tries to establish its error or demonstrate its falsity, he is but witnessing to its reality. ³Depression is then inevitable, for he has "proved," both to his pupil and himself, that it is their task to escape from what is real. ⁴And this can only be impossible. ⁵Reality is changeless. ⁶Magic thoughts are but illusions. ⁷Otherwise salvation would be only the same age-old impossible dream in but another form. ⁸Yet the dream of salvation has new content. ⁹It is not the form alone in which the difference lies.

2.   God's teachers' major lesson is to learn how to react to magic thoughts wholly without anger. ²Only in this way can they proclaim the truth about themselves. ³Through them, the Holy Spirit can now speak of the reality of the Son of God. ⁴Now He can remind the world of sinlessness, the one unchanged, unchangeable condition of all that God created. ⁵Now He can speak the Word of God to listening ears, and bring Christ's vision to eyes that see. ⁶Now is He free to teach all minds the truth of what they are, so they will gladly be returned to Him. ⁷And now is guilt forgiven, overlooked completely in His sight and in God's Word.

3.   Anger but screeches, "Guilt is real!" ²Reality is blotted out as this insane belief is taken as replacement for God's Word. ³The body's eyes now "see"; its ears alone can "hear." ⁴Its little space and tiny breath become the measure of reality. ⁵And truth becomes diminutive and meaningless. ⁶Correction has one answer to all this, and to the world that rests on this:

> ⁷*You but mistake interpretation for the truth. ⁸And you are wrong. ⁹But a mistake is not a sin, nor has reality been taken from its throne by your mistakes. ¹⁰God reigns forever, and His laws alone prevail upon you and upon the world. ¹¹His Love remains the only thing there is. ¹²Fear is illusion, for you are like Him.*

4. In order to heal, it thus becomes essential for the teacher of God to let all his own mistakes be corrected. [2]If he senses even the faintest hint of irritation in himself as he responds to anyone, let him instantly realize that he has made an interpretation that is not true. [3]Then let him turn within to his Eternal Guide, and let Him judge what the response should be. [4]So is he healed, and in his healing is his pupil healed with him. [5]The sole responsibility of God's teacher is to accept the Atonement for himself. [6]Atonement means correction, or the undoing of errors. [7]When this has been accomplished, the teacher of God becomes a miracle worker by definition. [8]His sins have been forgiven him, and he no longer condemns himself. [9]How can he then condemn anyone? [10]And who is there whom his forgiveness can fail to heal?

19. WHAT IS JUSTICE?

1.   Justice is the divine correction for injustice. ²Injustice is the basis for all the judgments of the world. ³Justice corrects the interpretations to which injustice gives rise, and cancels them out. ⁴Neither justice nor injustice exists in Heaven, for error is impossible and correction meaningless. ⁵In this world, however, forgiveness depends on justice, since all attack can only be unjust. ⁶Justice is the Holy Spirit's verdict upon the world. ⁷Except in His judgment justice is impossible, for no one in the world is capable of making only just interpretations and laying all injustices aside. ⁸If God's Son were fairly judged, there would be no need for salvation. ⁹The thought of separation would have been forever inconceivable.

2.   Justice, like its opposite, is an interpretation. ²It is, however, the one interpretation that leads to truth. ³This becomes possible because, while it is not true in itself, justice includes nothing that opposes truth. ⁴There is no inherent conflict between justice and truth; one is but the first small step in the direction of the other. ⁵The path becomes quite different as one goes along. ⁶Nor could all the magnificence, the grandeur of the scene and the enormous opening vistas that rise to meet one as the journey continues, be foretold from the outset. ⁷Yet even these, whose splendor reaches indescribable heights as one proceeds, fall short indeed of all that wait when the pathway ceases and time ends with it. ⁸But somewhere one must start. ⁹Justice is the beginning.

3.   All concepts of your brothers and yourself; all fears of future states and all concerns about the past, stem from injustice. ²Here is the lens which, held before the body's eyes, distorts perception and brings witness of the distorted world back to the mind that made the lens and holds it very dear. ³Selectively and arbitrarily is every concept of the world built up in just this way. ⁴"Sins" are perceived and justified by careful selectivity in which all thought of wholeness must be lost. ⁵Forgiveness has no place in such a scheme, for not one "sin" but seems forever true.

4.   Salvation is God's justice. ²It restores to your awareness the wholeness of the fragments you perceive as broken off and separate. ³And it is this that overcomes the fear of death. ⁴For separate fragments must decay and die, but wholeness is immortal. ⁵It remains forever and forever like its Creator, being one with

Him. ⁶God's Judgment is His justice. ⁷Onto this,—a Judgment wholly lacking in condemnation; an evaluation based entirely on love,—you have projected your injustice, giving God the lens of warped perception through which you look. ⁸Now it belongs to Him and not to you. ⁹You are afraid of Him, and do not see you hate and fear your Self as enemy.

5. Pray for God's justice, and do not confuse His mercy with your own insanity. ²Perception can make whatever picture the mind desires to see. ³Remember this. ⁴In this lies either Heaven or hell, as you elect. ⁵God's justice points to Heaven just because it is entirely impartial. ⁶It accepts all evidence that is brought before it, omitting nothing and assessing nothing as separate and apart from all the rest. ⁷From this one standpoint does it judge, and this alone. ⁸Here all attack and condemnation becomes meaningless and indefensible. ⁹Perception rests, the mind is still, and light returns again. ¹⁰Vision is now restored. ¹¹What had been lost has now been found. ¹²The peace of God descends on all the world, and we can see. ¹³And we can see!

20. WHAT IS THE PEACE OF GOD?

1. It has been said that there is a kind of peace that is not of this world. ²How is it recognized? ³How is it found? ⁴And being found, how can it be retained? ⁵Let us consider each of these questions separately, for each reflects a different step along the way.

2. First, how can the peace of God be recognized? ²God's peace is recognized at first by just one thing; in every way it is totally unlike all previous experiences. ³It calls to mind nothing that went before. ⁴It brings with it no past associations. ⁵It is a new thing entirely. ⁶There is a contrast, yes, between this thing and all the past. ⁷But strangely, it is not a contrast of true differences. ⁸The past just slips away, and in its place is everlasting quiet. ⁹Only that. ¹⁰The contrast first perceived has merely gone. ¹¹Quiet has reached to cover everything.

3. How is this quiet found? ²No one can fail to find it who but seeks out its conditions. ³God's peace can never come where anger is, for anger must deny that peace exists. ⁴Who sees anger as justified in any way or any circumstance proclaims that peace is meaningless, and must believe that it cannot exist. ⁵In this condition, peace cannot be found. ⁶Therefore, forgiveness is the necessary condition for finding the peace of God. ⁷More than this, given forgiveness there *must* be peace. ⁸For what except attack will lead to war? ⁹And what but peace is opposite to war? ¹⁰Here the initial contrast stands out clear and apparent. ¹¹Yet when peace is found, the war is meaningless. ¹²And it is conflict now that is perceived as nonexistent and unreal.

4. How is the peace of God retained, once it is found? ²Returning anger, in whatever form, will drop the heavy curtain once again, and the belief that peace cannot exist will certainly return. ³War is again accepted as the one reality. ⁴Now must you once again lay down your sword, although you do not recognize that you have picked it up again. ⁵But you will learn, as you remember even faintly now what happiness was yours without it, that you must have taken it again as your defense. ⁶Stop for a moment now and think of this: Is conflict what you want, or is God's peace the better choice? ⁷Which gives you more? ⁸A tranquil mind is not a little gift. ⁹Would you not rather live than choose to die?

5. Living is joy, but death can only weep. ²You see in death escape from what you made. ³But this you do not see; that you made

death, and it is but illusion of an end. ⁴Death cannot be escape, because it is not life in which the problem lies. ⁵Life has no opposite, for it is God. ⁶Life and death seem to be opposites because you have decided death ends life. ⁷Forgive the world, and you will understand that everything that God created cannot have an end, and nothing He did not create is real. ⁸In this one sentence is our course explained. ⁹In this one sentence is our practicing given its one direction. ¹⁰And in this one sentence is the Holy Spirit's whole curriculum specified exactly as it is.

6.   What is the peace of God? ²No more than this; the simple understanding that His Will is wholly without opposite. ³There is no thought that contradicts His Will, yet can be true. ⁴The contrast between His Will and yours but seemed to be reality. ⁵In truth there was no conflict, for His Will is yours. ⁶Now is the mighty Will of God Himself His gift to you. ⁷He does not seek to keep it for Himself. ⁸Why would you seek to keep your tiny frail imaginings apart from Him? ⁹The Will of God is one and all there is. ¹⁰This is your heritage. ¹¹The universe beyond the sun and stars, and all the thoughts of which you can conceive, belong to you. ¹²God's peace is the condition for His Will. ¹³Attain His peace, and you remember Him

21. WHAT IS THE ROLE OF WORDS IN HEALING?

1. Strictly speaking, words play no part at all in healing. ²The motivating factor is prayer, or asking. ³What you ask for you receive. ⁴But this refers to the prayer of the heart, not to the words you use in praying. ⁵Sometimes the words and the prayer are contradictory; sometimes they agree. ⁶It does not matter. ⁷God does not understand words, for they were made by separated minds to keep them in the illusion of separation. ⁸Words can be helpful, particularly for the beginner, in helping concentration and facilitating the exclusion, or at least the control, of extraneous thoughts. ⁹Let us not forget, however, that words are but symbols of symbols. ¹⁰They are thus twice removed from reality.

2. As symbols, words have quite specific references. ²Even when they seem most abstract, the picture that comes to mind is apt to be very concrete. ³Unless a specific referent does occur to the mind in conjunction with the word, the word has little or no practical meaning, and thus cannot help the healing process. ⁴The prayer of the heart does not really ask for concrete things. ⁵It always requests some kind of experience, the specific things asked for being the bringers of the desired experience in the opinion of the asker. ⁶The words, then, are symbols for the things asked for, but the things themselves but stand for the experiences that are hoped for.

3. The prayer for things of this world will bring experiences of this world. ²If the prayer of the heart asks for this, this will be given because this will be received. ³It is impossible that the prayer of the heart remain unanswered in the perception of the one who asks. ⁴If he asks for the impossible, if he wants what does not exist or seeks for illusions in his heart, all this becomes his own. ⁵The power of his decision offers it to him as he requests. ⁶Herein lie hell and Heaven. ⁷The sleeping Son of God has but this power left to him. ⁸It is enough. ⁹His words do not matter. ¹⁰Only the Word of God has any meaning, because it symbolizes that which has no human symbols at all. ¹¹The Holy Spirit alone understands what this Word stands for. ¹²And this, too, is enough.

4. Is the teacher of God, then, to avoid the use of words in his teaching? ²No, indeed! ³There are many who must be reached through words, being as yet unable to hear in silence. ⁴The teacher of God must, however, learn to use words in a new way.

⁵Gradually, he learns how to let his words be chosen for him by ceasing to decide for himself what he will say. ⁶This process is merely a special case of the lesson in the workbook that says, "I will step back and let Him lead the way." ⁷The teacher of God accepts the words which are offered him, and gives as he receives. ⁸He does not control the direction of his speaking. ⁹He listens and hears and speaks.

5. A major hindrance in this aspect of his learning is the teacher of God's fear about the validity of what he hears. ²And what he hears may indeed be quite startling. ³It may also seem to be quite irrelevant to the presented problem as he perceives it, and may, in fact, confront the teacher with a situation that appears to be very embarrassing to him. ⁴All these are judgments that have no value. ⁵They are his own, coming from a shabby self-perception which he would leave behind. ⁶Judge not the words that come to you, but offer them in confidence. ⁷They are far wiser than your own. ⁸God's teachers have God's Word behind their symbols. ⁹And He Himself gives to the words they use the power of His Spirit, raising them from meaningless symbols to the Call of Heaven itself.

22. HOW ARE HEALING AND ATONEMENT RELATED?

1. Healing and Atonement are not related; they are identical. ²There is no order of difficulty in miracles because there are no degrees of Atonement. ³It is the one complete concept possible in this world, because it is the source of a wholly unified perception. ⁴Partial Atonement is a meaningless idea, just as special areas of hell in Heaven are inconceivable. ⁵Accept Atonement and you are healed. ⁶Atonement is the Word of God. ⁷Accept His Word and what remains to make sickness possible? ⁸Accept His Word and every miracle has been accomplished. ⁹To forgive is to heal. ¹⁰The teacher of God has taken accepting the Atonement for himself as his only function. ¹¹What is there, then, he cannot heal? ¹²What miracle can be withheld from him?

2. The progress of the teacher of God may be slow or rapid, depending on whether he recognizes the Atonement's inclusiveness, or for a time excludes some problem areas from it. ²In some cases, there is a sudden and complete awareness of the perfect applicability of the lesson of the Atonement to all situations, but this is comparatively rare. ³The teacher of God may have accepted the function God has given him long before he has learned all that his acceptance holds out to him. ⁴It is only the end that is certain. ⁵Anywhere along the way, the necessary realization of inclusiveness may reach him. ⁶If the way seems long, let him be content. ⁷He has decided on the direction he wants to take. ⁸What more was asked of him? ⁹And having done what was required, would God withhold the rest?

3. That forgiveness is healing needs to be understood, if the teacher of God is to make progress. ²The idea that a body can be sick is a central concept in the ego's thought system. ³This thought gives the body autonomy, separates it from the mind, and keeps the idea of attack inviolate. ⁴If the body could be sick Atonement would be impossible. ⁵A body that can order a mind to do as it sees fit could merely take the place of God and prove salvation is impossible. ⁶What, then, is left to heal? ⁷The body has become lord of the mind. ⁸How could the mind be returned to the Holy Spirit unless the body is killed? ⁹And who would want salvation at such a price?

4. Certainly sickness does not appear to be a decision. ²Nor would anyone actually believe he wants to be sick. ³Perhaps he

can accept the idea in theory, but it is rarely if ever consistently applied to all specific forms of sickness, both in the individual's perception of himself and of all others as well. ⁴Nor is it at this level that the teacher of God calls forth the miracle of healing. ⁵He overlooks the mind *and* body, seeing only the face of Christ shining in front of him, correcting all mistakes and healing all perception. ⁶Healing is the result of the recognition, by God's teacher, of who it is that is in need of healing. ⁷This recognition has no special reference. ⁸It is true of all things that God created. ⁹In it are all illusions healed.

5.   When a teacher of God fails to heal, it is because he has forgotten Who he is. ²Another's sickness thus becomes his own. ³In allowing this to happen, he has identified with another's ego, and has thus confused him with a body. ⁴In so doing, he has refused to accept the Atonement for himself, and can hardly offer it to his brother in Christ's Name. ⁵He will, in fact, be unable to recognize his brother at all, for his Father did not create bodies, and so he is seeing in his brother only the unreal. ⁶Mistakes do not correct mistakes, and distorted perception does not heal. ⁷Step back now, teacher of God. ⁸You have been wrong. ⁹Lead not the way, for you have lost it. ¹⁰Turn quickly to your Teacher, and let yourself be healed.

6.   The offer of Atonement is universal. ²It is equally applicable to all individuals in all circumstances. ³And in it is the power to heal all individuals of all forms of sickness. ⁴Not to believe this is to be unfair to God, and thus unfaithful to Him. ⁵A sick person perceives himself as separate from God. ⁶Would you see him as separate from you? ⁷It is your task to heal the sense of separation that has made him sick. ⁸It is your function to recognize for him that what he believes about himself is not the truth. ⁹It is your forgiveness that must show him this. ¹⁰Healing is very simple. ¹¹Atonement is received and offered. ¹²Having been received, it must be accepted. ¹³It is in the receiving, then, that healing lies. ¹⁴All else must follow from this single purpose.

7.   Who can limit the power of God Himself? ²Who, then, can say which one can be healed of what, and what must remain beyond God's power to forgive? ³This is insanity indeed. ⁴It is not up to God's teachers to set limits upon Him, because it is not up to them to judge His Son. ⁵And to judge His Son is to limit his Father. ⁶Both are equally meaningless. ⁷Yet this will not be understood until God's teacher recognizes that they are the same mis-

take. [8]Herein does he receive Atonement, for he withdraws his judgment from the Son of God, accepting him as God created him. [9]No longer does he stand apart from God, determining where healing should be given and where it should be withheld. [10]Now can he say with God, "This is my beloved Son, created perfect and forever so."

23. DOES JESUS HAVE A SPECIAL PLACE IN HEALING?

1. God's gifts can rarely be received directly. ²Even the most advanced of God's teachers will give way to temptation in this world. ³Would it be fair if their pupils were denied healing because of this? ⁴The Bible says, "Ask in the Name of Jesus Christ." ⁵Is this merely an appeal to magic? ⁶A name does not heal, nor does an invocation call forth any special power. ⁷What does it mean to call on Jesus Christ? ⁸What does calling on his Name confer? ⁹Why is the appeal to him part of healing?

2. We have repeatedly said that one who has perfectly accepted the Atonement for himself can heal the world. ²Indeed, he has already done so. ³Temptation may recur to others, but never to this One. ⁴He has become the risen Son of God. ⁵He has overcome death because he has accepted Life. ⁶He has recognized himself as God created him, and in so doing he has recognized all living things as part of him. ⁷There is now no limit on his power, because it is the Power of God. ⁸So has his name become the Name of God, for he no longer sees himself as separate from Him.

3. What does this mean for you? ²It means that in remembering Jesus you are remembering God. ³The whole relationship of the Son to the Father lies in him. ⁴His part in the Sonship is also yours, and his completed learning guarantees your own success. ⁵Is he still available for help? ⁶What did he say about this? ⁷Remember his promises, and ask yourself honestly whether it is likely that he will fail to keep them. ⁸Can God fail His Son? ⁹And can one who is one with God be unlike Him? ¹⁰Who transcends the body has transcended limitation. ¹¹Would the greatest teacher be unavailable to those who follow him?

4. The Name of Jesus Christ as such is but a symbol. ²But it stands for love that is not of this world. ³It is a symbol that is safely used as a replacement for the many names of all the gods to which you pray. ⁴It becomes the shining symbol for the Word of God, so close to what it stands for that the little space between the two is lost, the moment that the Name is called to mind. ⁵Remembering the Name of Jesus Christ is to give thanks for all the gifts that God has given you. ⁶And gratitude to God becomes the way in which He is remembered, for love cannot be far behind a grateful heart and thankful mind. ⁷God enters easily, for these are the true conditions for your homecoming.

5.   Jesus has led the way. ²Why would you not be grateful to him? ³He has asked for love, but only that he might give it to you. ⁴You do not love yourself. ⁵But in his eyes your loveliness is so complete and flawless that he sees in it an image of his Father. ⁶You become the symbol of his Father here on earth. ⁷To you he looks for hope, because in you he sees no limit and no stain to mar your beautiful perfection. ⁸In his eyes Christ's vision shines in perfect constancy. ⁹He has remained with you. ¹⁰Would you not learn the lesson of salvation through his learning? ¹¹Why would you choose to start again, when he has made the journey for you?

6.   No one on earth can grasp what Heaven is, or what its one Creator really means. ²Yet we have witnesses. ³It is to them that wisdom should appeal. ⁴There have been those whose learning far exceeds what we can learn. ⁵Nor would we teach the limitations we have laid on us. ⁶No one who has become a true and dedicated teacher of God forgets his brothers. ⁷Yet what he can offer them is limited by what he learns himself. ⁸Then turn to one who laid all limits by, and went beyond the farthest reach of learning. ⁹He will take you with him, for he did not go alone. ¹⁰And you were with him then, as you are now.

7.   This course has come from him because his words have reached you in a language you can love and understand. ²Are other teachers possible, to lead the way to those who speak in different tongues and appeal to different symbols? ³Certainly there are. ⁴Would God leave anyone without a very present help in time of trouble; a savior who can symbolize Himself? ⁵Yet do we need a many-faceted curriculum, not because of content differences, but because symbols must shift and change to suit the need. ⁶Jesus has come to answer yours. ⁷In him you find God's Answer. ⁸Do you, then, teach with him, for he is with you; he is always here.

24. IS REINCARNATION SO?

1.   In the ultimate sense, reincarnation is impossible. ²There is no past or future, and the idea of birth into a body has no meaning either once or many times. ³Reincarnation cannot, then, be true in any real sense. ⁴Our only question should be, "Is the concept helpful?" ⁵And that depends, of course, on what it is used for. ⁶If it is used to strengthen the recognition of the eternal nature of life, it is helpful indeed. ⁷Is any other question about it really useful in lighting up the way? ⁸Like many other beliefs, it can be bitterly misused. ⁹At least, such misuse offers preoccupation and perhaps pride in the past. ¹⁰At worst, it induces inertia in the present. ¹¹In between, many kinds of folly are possible.

2.   Reincarnation would not, under any circumstances, be the problem to be dealt with *now*. ²If it were responsible for some of the difficulties the individual faces now, his task would still be only to escape from them now. ³If he is laying the groundwork for a future life, he can still work out his salvation only now. ⁴To some, there may be comfort in the concept, and if it heartens them its value is self-evident. ⁵It is certain, however, that the way to salvation can be found by those who believe in reincarnation and by those who do not. ⁶The idea cannot, therefore, be regarded as essential to the curriculum. ⁷There is always some risk in seeing the present in terms of the past. ⁸There is always some good in any thought which strengthens the idea that life and the body are not the same.

3.   For our purposes, it would not be helpful to take any definite stand on reincarnation. ²A teacher of God should be as helpful to those who believe in it as to those who do not. ³If a definite stand were required of him, it would merely limit his usefulness, as well as his own decision making. ⁴Our course is not concerned with any concept that is not acceptable to anyone, regardless of his formal beliefs. ⁵His ego will be enough for him to cope with, and it is not the part of wisdom to add sectarian controversies to his burdens. ⁶Nor would there be an advantage in his premature acceptance of the course merely because it advocates a long-held belief of his own.

4.   It cannot be too strongly emphasized that this course aims at a complete reversal of thought. ²When this is finally accomplished, issues such as the validity of reincarnation become meaningless.

³Until then, they are likely to be merely controversial. ⁴The teacher of God is, therefore, wise to step away from all such questions, for he has much to teach and learn apart from them. ⁵He should both learn and teach that theoretical issues but waste time, draining it away from its appointed purpose. ⁶If there are aspects to any concept or belief that will be helpful, he will be told about it. ⁷He will also be told how to use it. ⁸What more need he know?

5. Does this mean that the teacher of God should not believe in reincarnation himself, or discuss it with others who do? ²The answer is, certainly not! ³If he does believe in reincarnation, it would be a mistake for him to renounce the belief unless his internal Teacher so advised. ⁴And this is most unlikely. ⁵He might be advised that he is misusing the belief in some way that is detrimental to his pupil's advance or his own. ⁶Reinterpretation would then be recommended, because it is necessary. ⁷All that must be recognized, however, is that birth was not the beginning, and death is not the end. ⁸Yet even this much is not required of the beginner. ⁹He need merely accept the idea that what he knows is not necessarily all there is to learn. ¹⁰His journey has begun.

6. The emphasis of this course always remains the same;—it is at this moment that complete salvation is offered you, and it is at this moment that you can accept it. ²This is still your one responsibility. ³Atonement might be equated with total escape from the past and total lack of interest in the future. ⁴Heaven is here. ⁵There is nowhere else. ⁶Heaven is now. ⁷There is no other time. ⁸No teaching that does not lead to this is of concern to God's teachers. ⁹All beliefs will point to this if properly interpreted. ¹⁰In this sense, it can be said that their truth lies in their usefulness. ¹¹All beliefs that lead to progress should be honored. ¹²This is the sole criterion this course requires. ¹³No more than this is necessary.

25. ARE "PSYCHIC" POWERS DESIRABLE?

1. The answer to this question is much like the preceding one. ²There are, of course, no "unnatural" powers, and it is obviously merely an appeal to magic to make up a power that does not exist. ³It is equally obvious, however, that each individual has many abilities of which he is unaware. ⁴As his awareness increases, he may well develop abilities that seem quite startling to him. ⁵Yet nothing he can do can compare even in the slightest with the glorious surprise of remembering Who he is. ⁶Let all his learning and all his efforts be directed toward this one great final surprise, and he will not be content to be delayed by the little ones that may come to him on the way.

2. Certainly there are many "psychic" powers that are clearly in line with this course. ²Communication is not limited to the small range of channels the world recognizes. ³If it were, there would be little point in trying to teach salvation. ⁴It would be impossible to do so. ⁵The limits the world places on communication are the chief barriers to direct experience of the Holy Spirit, Whose Presence is always there and Whose Voice is available but for the hearing. ⁶These limits are placed out of fear, for without them the walls that surround all the separate places of the world would fall at the holy sound of His Voice. ⁷Who transcends these limits in any way is merely becoming more natural. ⁸He is doing nothing special, and there is no magic in his accomplishments.

3. The seemingly new abilities that may be gathered on the way can be very helpful. ²Given to the Holy Spirit, and used under His direction, they are valuable teaching aids. ³To this, the question of how they arise is irrelevant. ⁴The only important consideration is how they are used. ⁵Taking them as ends in themselves, no matter how this is done, will delay progress. ⁶Nor does their value lie in proving anything; achievements from the past, unusual attunement with the "unseen," or "special" favors from God. ⁷God gives no special favors, and no one has any powers that are not available to everyone. ⁸Only by tricks of magic are special powers "demonstrated."

4. Nothing that is genuine is used to deceive. ²The Holy Spirit is incapable of deception, and He can use only genuine abilities. ³What is used for magic is useless to Him. ⁴But what He uses cannot be used for magic. ⁵There is, however, a particular appeal

in unusual abilities that can be curiously tempting. [6]Here are strengths which the Holy Spirit wants and needs. [7]Yet the ego sees in these same strengths an opportunity to glorify itself. [8]Strengths turned to weakness are tragedy indeed. [9]Yet what is not given to the Holy Spirit must be given to weakness, for what is withheld from love is given to fear, and will be fearful in consequence.

5. Even those who no longer value the material things of the world may still be deceived by "psychic" powers. [2]As investment has been withdrawn from the world's material gifts, the ego has been seriously threatened. [3]It may still be strong enough to rally under this new temptation to win back strength by guile. [4]Many have not seen through the ego's defenses here, although they are not particularly subtle. [5]Yet, given a remaining wish to be deceived, deception is made easy. [6]Now the "power" is no longer a genuine ability, and cannot be used dependably. [7]It is almost inevitable that, unless the individual changes his mind about its purpose, he will bolster his "power's" uncertainties with increasing deception.

6. Any ability that anyone develops has the potentiality for good. [2]To this there is no exception. [3]And the more unusual and unexpected the power, the greater its potential usefulness. [4]Salvation has need of all abilities, for what the world would destroy the Holy Spirit would restore. [5]"Psychic" abilities have been used to call upon the devil, which merely means to strengthen the ego. [6]Yet here is also a great channel of hope and healing in the Holy Spirit's service. [7]Those who have developed "psychic" powers have simply let some of the limitations they laid upon their minds be lifted. [8]It can be but further limitations they lay upon themselves if they utilize their increased freedom for greater imprisonment. [9]The Holy Spirit needs these gifts, and those who offer them to Him and Him alone go with Christ's gratitude upon their hearts, and His holy sight not far behind.

26. CAN GOD BE REACHED DIRECTLY?

1. God indeed can be reached directly, for there is no distance between Him and His Son. ²His awareness is in everyone's memory, and His Word is written on everyone's heart. ³Yet this awareness and this memory can arise across the threshold of recognition only where all barriers to truth have been removed. ⁴In how many is this the case? ⁵Here, then, is the role of God's teachers. ⁶They, too, have not attained the necessary understanding as yet, but they have joined with others. ⁷This is what sets them apart from the world. ⁸And it is this that enables others to leave the world with them. ⁹Alone they are nothing. ¹⁰But in their joining is the Power of God.

2. There are those who have reached God directly, retaining no trace of worldly limits and remembering their own Identity perfectly. ²These might be called the Teachers of teachers because, although they are no longer visible, their image can yet be called upon. ³And they will appear when and where it is helpful for them to do so. ⁴To those to whom such appearances would be frightening, they give their ideas. ⁵No one can call on them in vain. ⁶Nor is there anyone of whom they are unaware. ⁷All needs are known to them, and all mistakes are recognized and overlooked by them. ⁸The time will come when this is understood. ⁹And meanwhile, they give all their gifts to the teachers of God who look to them for help, asking all things in their Name and in no other.

3. Sometimes a teacher of God may have a brief experience of direct union with God. ²In this world, it is almost impossible that this endure. ³It can, perhaps, be won after much devotion and dedication, and then be maintained for much of the time on earth. ⁴But this is so rare that it cannot be considered a realistic goal. ⁵If it happens, so be it. ⁶If it does not happen, so be it as well. ⁷All worldly states must be illusory. ⁸If God were reached directly in sustained awareness, the body would not be long maintained. ⁹Those who have laid the body down merely to extend their helpfulness to those remaining behind are few indeed. ¹⁰And they need helpers who are still in bondage and still asleep, so that by their awakening can God's Voice be heard.

4. Do not despair, then, because of limitations. ²It is your function to escape from them, but not to be without them. ³If you would

be heard by those who suffer, you must speak their language. [4]If you would be a savior, you must understand what needs to be escaped. [5]Salvation is not theoretical. [6]Behold the problem, ask for the answer, and then accept it when it comes. [7]Nor will its coming be long delayed. [8]All the help you can accept will be provided, and not one need you have will not be met. [9]Let us not, then, be too concerned with goals for which you are not ready. [10]God takes you where you are and welcomes you. [11]What more could you desire, when this is all you need?

27. WHAT IS DEATH?

1. Death is the central dream from which all illusions stem. ²Is it not madness to think of life as being born, aging, losing vitality, and dying in the end? ³We have asked this question before, but now we need to consider it more carefully. ⁴It is the one fixed, unchangeable belief of the world that all things in it are born only to die. ⁵This is regarded as "the way of nature," not to be raised to question, but to be accepted as the "natural" law of life. ⁶The cyclical, the changing and unsure; the undependable and the unsteady, waxing and waning in a certain way upon a certain path,—all this is taken as the Will of God. ⁷And no one asks if a benign Creator could will this.

2. In this perception of the universe as God created it, it would be impossible to think of Him as loving. ²For who has decreed that all things pass away, ending in dust and disappointment and despair, can but be feared. ³He holds your little life in his hand but by a thread, ready to break it off without regret or care, perhaps today. ⁴Or if he waits, yet is the ending certain. ⁵Who loves such a god knows not of love, because he has denied that life is real. ⁶Death has become life's symbol. ⁷His world is now a battleground, where contradiction reigns and opposites make endless war. ⁸Where there is death is peace impossible.

3. Death is the symbol of the fear of God. ²His Love is blotted out in the idea, which holds it from awareness like a shield held up to obscure the sun. ³The grimness of the symbol is enough to show it cannot coexist with God. ⁴It holds an image of the Son of God in which he is "laid to rest" in devastation's arms, where worms wait to greet him and to last a little while by his destruction. ⁵Yet the worms as well are doomed to be destroyed as certainly. ⁶And so do all things live because of death. ⁷Devouring is nature's "law of life." ⁸God is insane, and fear alone is real.

4. The curious belief that there is part of dying things that may go on apart from what will die, does not proclaim a loving God nor re-establish any grounds for trust. ²If death is real for anything, there is no life. ³Death denies life. ⁴But if there is reality in life, death is denied. ⁵No compromise in this is possible. ⁶There is either a god of fear or One of Love. ⁷The world attempts a thousand compromises, and will attempt a thousand more. ⁸Not one can be acceptable to God's teachers, because not one could be

acceptable to God. ⁹He did not make death because He did not make fear. ¹⁰Both are equally meaningless to Him.

5. The "reality" of death is firmly rooted in the belief that God's Son is a body. ²And if God created bodies, death would indeed be real. ³But God would not be loving. ⁴There is no point at which the contrast between the perception of the real world and that of the world of illusions becomes more sharply evident. ⁵Death is indeed the death of God, if He is Love. ⁶And now His Own creation must stand in fear of Him. ⁷He is not Father, but destroyer. ⁸He is not Creator, but avenger. ⁹Terrible His Thoughts and fearful His image. ¹⁰To look on His creations is to die.

6. "And the last to be overcome will be death." ²Of course! ³Without the idea of death there is no world. ⁴All dreams will end with this one. ⁵This is salvation's final goal; the end of all illusions. ⁶And in death are all illusions born. ⁷What can be born of death and still have life? ⁸But what is born of God and still can die? ⁹The inconsistencies, the compromises and the rituals the world fosters in its vain attempts to cling to death and yet to think love real are mindless magic, ineffectual and meaningless. ¹⁰God is, and in Him all created things must be eternal. ¹¹Do you not see that otherwise He has an opposite, and fear would be as real as love?

7. Teacher of God, your one assignment could be stated thus: Accept no compromise in which death plays a part. ²Do not believe in cruelty, nor let attack conceal the truth from you. ³What seems to die has but been misperceived and carried to illusion. ⁴Now it becomes your task to let the illusion be carried to the truth. ⁵Be steadfast but in this; be not deceived by the "reality" of any changing form. ⁶Truth neither moves nor wavers nor sinks down to death and dissolution. ⁷And what is the end of death? ⁸Nothing but this; the realization that the Son of God is guiltless now and forever. ⁹Nothing but this. ¹⁰But do not let yourself forget it is not less than this.

28. WHAT IS THE RESURRECTION?

1. Very simply, the resurrection is the overcoming or surmounting of death. ²It is a reawakening or a rebirth; a change of mind about the meaning of the world. ³It is the acceptance of the Holy Spirit's interpretation of the world's purpose; the acceptance of the Atonement for oneself. ⁴It is the end of dreams of misery, and the glad awareness of the Holy Spirit's final dream. ⁵It is the recognition of the gifts of God. ⁶It is the dream in which the body functions perfectly, having no function except communication. ⁷It is the lesson in which learning ends, for it is consummated and surpassed with this. ⁸It is the invitation to God to take His final step. ⁹It is the relinquishment of all other purposes, all other interests, all other wishes and all other concerns. ¹⁰It is the single desire of the Son for the Father.

2. The resurrection is the denial of death, being the assertion of life. ²Thus is all the thinking of the world reversed entirely. ³Life is now recognized as salvation, and pain and misery of any kind perceived as hell. ⁴Love is no longer feared, but gladly welcomed. ⁵Idols have disappeared, and the remembrance of God shines unimpeded across the world. ⁶Christ's face is seen in every living thing, and nothing is held in darkness, apart from the light of forgiveness. ⁷There is no sorrow still upon the earth. ⁸The joy of Heaven has come upon it.

3. Here the curriculum ends. ²From here on, no directions are needed. ³Vision is wholly corrected and all mistakes undone. ⁴Attack is meaningless and peace has come. ⁵The goal of the curriculum has been achieved. ⁶Thoughts turn to Heaven and away from hell. ⁷All longings are satisfied, for what remains unanswered or incomplete? ⁸The last illusion spreads across the world, forgiving all things and replacing all attack. ⁹The whole reversal is accomplished. ¹⁰Nothing is left to contradict the Word of God. ¹¹There is no opposition to the truth. ¹²And now the truth can come at last. ¹³How quickly will it come as it is asked to enter and envelop such a world!

4. All living hearts are tranquil with a stir of deep anticipation, for the time of everlasting things is now at hand. ²There is no death. ³The Son of God is free. ⁴And in his freedom is the end of fear. ⁵No hidden places now remain on earth to shelter sick illusions, dreams of fear and misperceptions of the universe. ⁶All things are

seen in light, and in the light their purpose is transformed and understood. ⁷And we, God's children, rise up from the dust and look upon our perfect sinlessness. ⁸The song of Heaven sounds around the world, as it is lifted up and brought to truth.

5.   Now there are no distinctions. ²Differences have disappeared and Love looks on Itself. ³What further sight is needed? ⁴What remains that vision could accomplish? ⁵We have seen the face of Christ, His sinlessness, His Love behind all forms, beyond all purposes. ⁶Holy are we because His holiness has set us free indeed! ⁷And we accept His holiness as ours; as it is. ⁸As God created us so will we be forever and forever, and we wish for nothing but His Will to be our own. ⁹Illusions of another will are lost, for unity of purpose has been found.

6.   These things await us all, but we are not prepared as yet to welcome them with joy. ²As long as any mind remains possessed of evil dreams, the thought of hell is real. ³God's teachers have the goal of wakening the minds of those asleep, and seeing there the vision of Christ's face to take the place of what they dream. ⁴The thought of murder is replaced with blessing. ⁵Judgment is laid by, and given Him Whose function judgment is. ⁶And in His final judgment is restored the truth about the holy Son of God. ⁷He is redeemed, for he has heard God's Word and understood its meaning. ⁸He is free because he let God's Voice proclaim the truth. ⁹And all he sought before to crucify are resurrected with him, by his side, as he prepares with them to meet his God.

29. AS FOR THE REST...

1.   This manual is not intended to answer all questions that both teacher and pupil may raise. ²In fact, it covers only a few of the more obvious ones, in terms of a brief summary of some of the major concepts in the text and workbook. ³It is not a substitute for either, but merely a supplement. ⁴While it is called a manual for teachers, it must be remembered that only time divides teacher and pupil, so that the difference is temporary by definition. ⁵In some cases, it may be helpful for the pupil to read the manual first. ⁶Others might do better to begin with the workbook. ⁷Still others may need to start at the more abstract level of the text.

2.   Which is for which? ²Who would profit more from prayers alone? ³Who needs but a smile, being as yet unready for more? ⁴No one should attempt to answer these questions alone. ⁵Surely no teacher of God has come this far without realizing that. ⁶The curriculum is highly individualized, and all aspects are under the Holy Spirit's particular care and guidance. ⁷Ask and He will answer. ⁸The responsibility is His, and He alone is fit to assume it. ⁹To do so is His function. ¹⁰To refer the questions to Him is yours. ¹¹Would you want to be responsible for decisions about which you understand so little? ¹²Be glad you have a Teacher Who cannot make a mistake. ¹³His answers are always right. ¹⁴Would you say that of yours?

3.   There is another advantage,—and a very important one,—in referring decisions to the Holy Spirit with increasing frequency. ²Perhaps you have not thought of this aspect, but its centrality is obvious. ³To follow the Holy Spirit's guidance is to let yourself be absolved of guilt. ⁴It is the essence of the Atonement. ⁵It is the core of the curriculum. ⁶The imagined usurping of functions not your own is the basis of fear. ⁷The whole world you see reflects the illusion that you have done so, making fear inevitable. ⁸To return the function to the One to Whom it belongs is thus the escape from fear. ⁹And it is this that lets the memory of love return to you. ¹⁰Do not, then, think that following the Holy Spirit's guidance is necessary merely because of your own inadequacies. ¹¹It is the way out of hell for you.

4.   Here again is the paradox often referred to in the course. ²To say, "Of myself I can do nothing" is to gain all power. ³And yet it is but a seeming paradox. ⁴As God created you, you *have* all

power. ⁵The image you made of yourself has none. ⁶The Holy Spirit knows the truth about you. ⁷The image you made does not. ⁸Yet, despite its obvious and complete ignorance, this image assumes it knows all things because you have given that belief to it. ⁹Such is your teaching, and the teaching of the world that was made to uphold it. ¹⁰But the Teacher Who knows the truth has not forgotten it. ¹¹His decisions bring benefit to all, being wholly devoid of attack. ¹²And therefore incapable of arousing guilt.

5. Who assumes a power that he does not possess is deceiving himself. ²Yet to accept the power given him by God is but to acknowledge his Creator and accept His gifts. ³And His gifts have no limit. ⁴To ask the Holy Spirit to decide for you is simply to accept your true inheritance. ⁵Does this mean that you cannot say anything without consulting Him? ⁶No, indeed! ⁷That would hardly be practical, and it is the practical with which this course is most concerned. ⁸If you have made it a habit to ask for help when and where you can, you can be confident that wisdom will be given you when you need it. ⁹Prepare for this each morning, remember God when you can throughout the day, ask the Holy Spirit's help when it is feasible to do so, and thank Him for His guidance at night. ¹⁰And your confidence will be well founded indeed.

6. Never forget that the Holy Spirit does not depend on your words. ²He understands the requests of your heart, and answers them. ³Does this mean that, while attack remains attractive to you, He will respond with evil? ⁴Hardly! ⁵For God has given Him the power to translate your prayers of the heart into His language. ⁶He understands that an attack is a call for help. ⁷And He responds with help accordingly. ⁸God would be cruel if He let your words replace His Own. ⁹A loving father does not let his child harm himself, or choose his own destruction. ¹⁰He may ask for injury, but his father will protect him still. ¹¹And how much more than this does your Father love His Son?

7. Remember you are His completion and His Love. ²Remember your weakness is His strength. ³But do not read this hastily or wrongly. ⁴If His strength is in you, what you perceive as your weakness is but illusion. ⁵And He has given you the means to prove it so. ⁶Ask all things of His Teacher, and all things are given you. ⁷Not in the future but immediately; now. ⁸God does not wait, for waiting implies time and He is timeless. ⁹Forget your foolish images, your sense of frailty and your fear of harm, your

dreams of danger and selected "wrongs." [10]God knows but His Son, and as he was created so he is. [11]In confidence I place you in His Hands, and I give thanks for you that this is so.

8. And now in all your doings be you blessed.
   [2]God turns to you for help to save the world.
   [3]Teacher of God, His thanks He offers you,
   And all the world stands silent in the grace
   You bring from Him. [4]You are the Son He loves,
   And it is given you to be the means
   Through which His Voice is heard around the world,
   To close all things of time; to end the sight
   Of all things visible; and to undo
   All things that change. [5]Through you is ushered in
   A world unseen, unheard, yet truly there.
   [6]Holy are you, and in your light the world
   Reflects your holiness, for you are not
   Alone and friendless. [7]I give thanks for you,
   And join your efforts on behalf of God,
   Knowing they are on my behalf as well,
   And for all those who walk to God with me.

   [8]AMEN

CLARIFICATION OF TERMS

INTRODUCTION

1. This is not a course in philosophical speculation, nor is it concerned with precise terminology. ²It is concerned only with Atonement, or the correction of perception. ³The means of the Atonement is forgiveness. ⁴The structure of "individual consciousness" is essentially irrelevant because it is a concept representing the "original error" or the "original sin." ⁵To study the error itself does not lead to correction, if you are indeed to succeed in overlooking the error. ⁶And it is just this process of overlooking at which the course aims.

2. All terms are potentially controversial, and those who seek controversy will find it. ²Yet those who seek clarification will find it as well. ³They must, however, be willing to overlook controversy, recognizing that it is a defense against truth in the form of a delaying maneuver. ⁴Theological considerations as such are necessarily controversial, since they depend on belief and can therefore be accepted or rejected. ⁵A universal theology is impossible, but a universal experience is not only possible but necessary. ⁶It is this experience toward which the course is directed. ⁷Here alone consistency becomes possible because here alone uncertainty ends.

3. This course remains within the ego framework, where it is needed. ²It is not concerned with what is beyond all error because it is planned only to set the direction towards it. ³Therefore it uses words, which are symbolic, and cannot express what lies beyond symbols. ⁴It is merely the ego that questions because it is only the ego that doubts. ⁵The course merely gives another answer, once a question has been raised. ⁶However, this answer does not attempt to resort to inventiveness or ingenuity. ⁷These are attributes of the ego. ⁸*The course is simple.* ⁹It has one function and one goal. ¹⁰Only in that does it remain wholly consistent because only that can *be* consistent.

4. The ego will demand many answers that this course does not give. ²It does not recognize as questions the mere form of a question to which an answer is impossible. ³The ego may ask, "How did the impossible occur?", "To what did the impossible happen?", and may ask this in many forms. ⁴Yet there is no answer; only an experience. ⁵Seek only this, and do not let theology delay you.

5. You will notice that the emphasis on structural issues in the

course is brief and early. [2]Afterwards and soon, it drops away to make way for the central teaching. [3]Since you have asked for clarification, however, these are some of the terms that are used.

1. MIND – SPIRIT

1.   The term *mind* is used to represent the activating agent of spirit, supplying its creative energy. [2]When the term is capitalized it refers to God or Christ (i.e., the Mind of God or the Mind of Christ). [3]*Spirit* is the Thought of God which He created like Himself. [4]The unified spirit is God's one Son, or Christ.

2.   In this world, because the mind is split, the Sons of God appear to be separate. [2]Nor do their minds seem to be joined. [3]In this illusory state, the concept of an "individual mind" seems to be meaningful. [4]It is therefore described in the course *as if* it has two parts; spirit and ego.

3.   Spirit is the part that is still in contact with God through the Holy Spirit, Who abides in this part but sees the other part as well. [2]The term "soul" is not used except in direct biblical quotations because of its highly controversial nature. [3]It would, however, be an equivalent of "spirit," with the understanding that, being of God, it is eternal and was never born.

4.   The other part of the mind is entirely illusory and makes only illusions. [2]Spirit retains the potential for creating, but its Will, which is God's, seems to be imprisoned while the mind is not unified. [3]Creation continues unabated because that is the Will of God. [4]This Will is always unified and therefore has no meaning in this world. [5]It has no opposite and no degrees.

5.   The mind can be right or wrong, depending on the voice to which it listens. [2]*Right-mindedness* listens to the Holy Spirit, forgives the world, and through Christ's vision sees the real world in its place. [3]This is the final vision, the last perception, the condition in which God takes the final step Himself. [4]Here time and illusions end together.

6.   *Wrong-mindedness* listens to the ego and makes illusions; perceiving sin and justifying anger, and seeing guilt, disease and death as real. [2]Both this world and the real world are illusions because right-mindedness merely overlooks, or forgives, what never happened. [3]Therefore it is not the *One-mindedness* of the Christ Mind, Whose Will is one with God's.

7.   In this world the only remaining freedom is the freedom of choice; always between two choices or two voices. [2]Will is not involved in perception at any level, and has nothing to do with choice. [3]*Consciousness* is the receptive mechanism, receiving mes-

sages from above or below; from the Holy Spirit or the ego. [4]Consciousness has levels and awareness can shift quite dramatically, but it cannot transcend the perceptual realm. [5]At its highest it becomes aware of the real world, and can be trained to do so increasingly. [6]Yet the very fact that it has levels and can be trained demonstrates that it cannot reach knowledge.

2. THE EGO – THE MIRACLE

1. Illusions will not last. ²Their death is sure and this alone is certain in their world. ³It is the ego's world because of this. ⁴What is the *ego*? ⁵But a dream of what you really are. ⁶A thought you are apart from your Creator and a wish to be what He created not. ⁷It is a thing of madness, not reality at all. ⁸A name for namelessness is all it is. ⁹A symbol of impossibility; a choice for options that do not exist. ¹⁰We name it but to help us understand that it is nothing but an ancient thought that what is made has immortality. ¹¹But what could come of this except a dream which, like all dreams, can only end in death?

2. What is the ego? ²Nothingness, but in a form that seems like something. ³In a world of form the ego cannot be denied for it alone seems real. ⁴Yet could God's Son as He created him abide in form or in a world of form? ⁵Who asks you to define the ego and explain how it arose can be but he who thinks it real, and seeks by definition to ensure that its illusive nature is concealed behind the words that seem to make it so.

3. There is no definition for a lie that serves to make it true. ²Nor can there be a truth that lies conceal effectively. ³The ego's unreality is not denied by words nor is its meaning clear because its nature seems to have a form. ⁴Who can define the undefinable? ⁵And yet there is an answer even here.

4. We cannot really make a definition for what the ego is, but we *can* say what it is not. ²And this is shown to us with perfect clarity. ³It is from this that we deduce all that the ego is. ⁴Look at its opposite and you can see the only answer that is meaningful.

5. The ego's opposite in every way,—in origin, effect and consequence—we call a miracle. ²And here we find all that is not the ego in this world. ³Here is the ego's opposite and here alone we look on what the ego was, for here we see all that it seemed to do, and cause and its effects must still be one.

6. Where there was darkness now we see the light. ²What is the ego? ³What the darkness was. ⁴Where is the ego? ⁵Where the darkness was. ⁶What is it now and where can it be found? ⁷Nothing and nowhere. ⁸Now the light has come: its opposite has gone without a trace. ⁹Where evil was there now is holiness. ¹⁰What is the ego? ¹¹What the evil was. ¹²Where is the ego? ¹³In an evil dream that but seemed real while you were dreaming it. ¹⁴Where

there was crucifixion stands God's Son. [15]What is the ego? [16]Who has need to ask? [17]Where is the ego? [18]Who has need to seek for an illusion now that dreams are gone?

7. What is a *miracle*? [2]A dream as well. [3]But look at all the aspects of *this* dream and you will never question any more. [4]Look at the kindly world you see extend before you as you walk in gentleness. [5]Look at the helpers all along the way you travel, happy in the certainty of Heaven and the surety of peace. [6]And look an instant, too, on what you left behind at last and finally passed by.

8. This was the ego—all the cruel hate, the need for vengeance and the cries of pain, the fear of dying and the urge to kill, the brotherless illusion and the self that seemed alone in all the universe. [2]This terrible mistake about yourself the miracle corrects as gently as a loving mother sings her child to rest. [3]Is not a song like this what you would hear? [4]Would it not answer all you thought to ask, and even make the question meaningless?

9. Your questions have no answer, being made to still God's Voice, Which asks of everyone one question only: "Are you ready yet to help Me save the world?" [2]Ask this instead of what the ego is, and you will see a sudden brightness cover up the world the ego made. [3]No miracle is now withheld from anyone. [4]The world is saved from what you thought it was. [5]And what it is, is wholly uncondemned and wholly pure.

10. The miracle forgives; the ego damns. [2]Neither need be defined except by this. [3]Yet could a definition be more sure, or more in line with what salvation is? [4]Problem and answer lie together here, and having met at last the choice is clear. [5]Who chooses hell when it is recognized? [6]And who would not go on a little while when it is given him to understand the way is short and Heaven is his goal?

3. FORGIVENESS – THE FACE OF CHRIST

1.   *Forgiveness* is for God and toward God but not of Him. ²It is impossible to think of anything He created that could need forgiveness. ³Forgiveness, then, is an illusion, but because of its purpose, which is the Holy Spirit's, it has one difference. ⁴Unlike all other illusions it leads away from error and not towards it.

2.   Forgiveness might be called a kind of happy fiction; a way in which the unknowing can bridge the gap between their perception and the truth. ²They cannot go directly from perception to knowledge because they do not think it is their will to do so. ³This makes God appear to be an enemy instead of what He really is. ⁴And it is just this insane perception that makes them unwilling merely to rise up and to return to Him in peace.

3.   And so they need an illusion of help because they are helpless; a Thought of peace because they are in conflict. ²God knows what His Son needs before he asks. ³He is not at all concerned with form, but having given the content it is His Will that it be understood. ⁴And that suffices. ⁵The form adapts itself to need; the content is unchanging, as eternal as its Creator.

4.   *The face of Christ* has to be seen before the memory of God can return. ²The reason is obvious. ³Seeing the face of Christ involves perception. ⁴No one can look on knowledge. ⁵But the face of Christ is the great symbol of forgiveness. ⁶It is salvation. ⁷It is the symbol of the real world. ⁸Whoever looks on this no longer sees the world. ⁹He is as near to Heaven as is possible outside the gate. ¹⁰Yet from this gate it is no more than just a step inside. ¹¹It is the final step. ¹²And this we leave to God.

5.   Forgiveness is a symbol, too, but as the symbol of His Will alone it cannot be divided. ²And so the Unity that it reflects becomes His Will. ³It is the only thing still in the world in part, and yet the bridge to Heaven.

6.   God's Will is all there is. ²We can but go from nothingness to everything; from hell to Heaven. ³Is this a journey? ⁴No, not in truth, for truth goes nowhere. ⁵But illusions shift from place to place; from time to time. ⁶The final step is also but a shift. ⁷As a perception it is part unreal. ⁸And yet this part will vanish. ⁹What remains is peace eternal and the Will of God.

7.   There are no wishes now for wishes change. ²Even the wished-for can become unwelcome. ³That must be so because the ego

cannot be at peace. [4]But Will is constant, as the gift of God. [5]And what He gives is always like Himself. [6]This is the purpose of the face of Christ. [7]It is the gift of God to save His Son. [8]But look on this and you have been forgiven.

8.   How lovely does the world become in just that single instant when you see the truth about yourself reflected there. [2]Now you are sinless and behold your sinlessness. [3]Now you are holy and perceive it so. [4]And now the mind returns to its Creator; the joining of the Father and the Son, the Unity of unities that stands behind all joining but beyond them all. [5]God is not seen but only understood. [6]His Son is not attacked but recognized.

4. TRUE PERCEPTION – KNOWLEDGE

1.   The world you see is an illusion of a world. [2]God did not create it, for what He creates must be eternal as Himself. [3]Yet there is nothing in the world you see that will endure forever. [4]Some things will last in time a little while longer than others. [5]But the time will come when all things visible will have an end.

2.   The body's eyes are therefore not the means by which the real world can be seen, for the illusions that they look upon must lead to more illusions of reality. [2]And so they do. [3]For everything they see not only will not last, but lends itself to thoughts of sin and guilt. [4]While everything that God created is forever without sin and therefore is forever without guilt.

3.   Knowledge is not the remedy for false perception since, being another level, they can never meet. [2]The one correction possible for false perception must be *true perception*. [3]It will not endure. [4]But for the time it lasts it comes to heal. [5]For true perception is a remedy with many names. [6]Forgiveness, salvation, Atonement, true perception, all are one. [7]They are the one beginning, with the end to lead to Oneness far beyond themselves. [8]True perception is the means by which the world is saved from sin, for sin does not exist. [9]And it is this that true perception sees.

4.   The world stands like a block before Christ's face. [2]But true perception looks on it as nothing more than just a fragile veil, so easily dispelled that it can last no longer than an instant. [3]It is seen at last for only what it is. [4]And now it cannot fail to disappear, for now there is an empty place made clean and ready. [5]Where destruction was perceived the face of Christ appears, and in that instant is the world forgot, with time forever ended as the world spins into nothingness from where it came.

5.   A world forgiven cannot last. [2]It was the home of bodies. [3]But forgiveness looks past bodies. [4]This is its holiness; this is how it heals. [5]The world of bodies is the world of sin, for only if there were a body is sin possible. [6]From sin comes guilt as surely as forgiveness takes all guilt away. [7]And once all guilt is gone what more remains to keep a separated world in place? [8]For place has gone as well, along with time. [9]Only the body makes the world seem real, for being separate it could not remain where separation is impossible. [10]Forgiveness proves it is impossible because it sees it not. [11]And what you then will overlook will not be under-

standable to you, just as its presence once had been your certainty.
6.   This is the shift that true perception brings: What was projected out is seen within, and there forgiveness lets it disappear. ²For there the altar to the Son is set, and there his Father is remembered. ³Here are all illusions brought to truth and laid upon the altar. ⁴What is seen outside must lie beyond forgiveness, for it seems to be forever sinful. ⁵Where is hope while sin is seen as outside? ⁶What remedy can guilt expect? ⁷But seen within your mind, guilt and forgiveness for an instant lie together, side by side, upon one altar. ⁸There at last are sickness and its single remedy joined in one healing brightness. ⁹God has come to claim His Own. ¹⁰Forgiveness is complete.

7.   And now God's *knowledge*, changeless, certain, pure and wholly understandable, enters its kingdom. ²Gone is perception, false and true alike. ³Gone is forgiveness, for its task is done. ⁴And gone are bodies in the blazing light upon the altar to the Son of God. ⁵God knows it is His Own, as it is his. ⁶And here they join, for here the face of Christ has shone away time's final instant, and now is the last perception of the world without a purpose and without a cause. ⁷For where God's memory has come at last there is no journey, no belief in sin, no walls, no bodies, and the grim appeal of guilt and death is there snuffed out forever.

8.   O my brothers, if you only knew the peace that will envelop you and hold you safe and pure and lovely in the Mind of God, you could but rush to meet Him where His altar is. ²Hallowed your name and His, for they are joined here in this holy place. ³Here He leans down to lift you up to Him, out of illusions into holiness; out of the world and to eternity; out of all fear and given back to love.

5. JESUS – CHRIST

1.   There is no need for help to enter Heaven for you have never left. ²But there is need for help beyond yourself as you are circumscribed by false beliefs of your Identity, Which God alone established in reality. ³Helpers are given you in many forms, although upon the altar they are one. ⁴Beyond each one there is a Thought of God, and this will never change. ⁵But they have names which differ for a time, for time needs symbols, being itself unreal. ⁶Their names are legion, but we will not go beyond the names the course itself employs. ⁷God does not help because He knows no need. ⁸But He creates all Helpers of His Son while he believes his fantasies are true. ⁹Thank God for them for they will lead you home.

2.   The name of *Jesus* is the name of one who was a man but saw the face of Christ in all his brothers and remembered God. ²So he became identified with *Christ*, a man no longer, but at one with God. ³The man was an illusion, for he seemed to be a separate being, walking by himself, within a body that appeared to hold his self from Self, as all illusions do. ⁴Yet who can save unless he sees illusions and then identifies them as what they are? ⁵Jesus remains a Savior because he saw the false without accepting it as true. ⁶And Christ needed his form that He might appear to men and save them from their own illusions.

3.   In his complete identification with the Christ—the perfect Son of God, His one creation and His happiness, forever like Himself and one with Him—Jesus became what all of you must be. ²He led the way for you to follow him. ³He leads you back to God because he saw the road before him, and he followed it. ⁴He made a clear distinction, still obscure to you, between the false and true. ⁵He offered you a final demonstration that it is impossible to kill God's Son; nor can his life in any way be changed by sin and evil, malice, fear or death.

4.   And therefore all your sins have been forgiven because they carried no effects at all. ²And so they were but dreams. ³Arise with him who showed you this because you owe him this who shared your dreams that they might be dispelled. ⁴And shares them still, to be at one with you.

5.   Is he the Christ? ²O yes, along with you. ³His little life on earth was not enough to teach the mighty lesson that he learned for all

of you. ⁴He will remain with you to lead you from the hell you made to God. ⁵And when you join your will with his, your sight will be his vision, for the eyes of Christ are shared. ⁶Walking with him is just as natural as walking with a brother whom you knew since you were born, for such indeed he is. ⁷Some bitter idols have been made of him who would be only brother to the world. ⁸Forgive him your illusions, and behold how dear a brother he would be to you. ⁹For he will set your mind at rest at last and carry it with you unto your God.

6.   Is he God's only Helper? ²No, indeed. ³For Christ takes many forms with different names until their oneness can be recognized. ⁴But Jesus is for you the bearer of Christ's single message of the Love of God. ⁵You need no other. ⁶It is possible to read his words and benefit from them without accepting him into your life. ⁷Yet he would help you yet a little more if you will share your pains and joys with him, and leave them both to find the peace of God. ⁸Yet still it is his lesson most of all that he would have you learn, and it is this:

> ⁹*There is no death because the Son of God is like his Father.* ¹⁰*Nothing you can do can change Eternal Love.* ¹¹*Forget your dreams of sin and guilt, and come with me instead to share the resurrection of God's Son.* ¹²*And bring with you all those whom He has sent to you to care for as I care for you.*

6. THE HOLY SPIRIT

1. Jesus is the manifestation of the *Holy Spirit*, Whom he called down upon the earth after he ascended into Heaven, or became completely identified with the Christ, the Son of God as He created Him. [2]The Holy Spirit, being a creation of the One Creator, creating with Him and in His likeness or spirit, is eternal and has never changed. [3]He was "called down upon the earth" in the sense that it was now possible to accept Him and to hear His Voice. [4]His is the Voice for God, and has therefore taken form. [5]This form is not His reality, which God alone knows along with Christ, His real Son, Who is part of Him.

2. The Holy Spirit is described throughout the course as giving us the answer to the separation and bringing the plan of the Atonement to us, establishing our particular part in it and showing us exactly what it is. [2]He has established Jesus as the leader in carrying out His plan since he was the first to complete his own part perfectly. [3]All power in Heaven and earth is therefore given him and he will share it with you when you have completed yours. [4]The Atonement principle was given to the Holy Spirit long before Jesus set it in motion.

3. The Holy Spirit is described as the remaining communication link between God and His separated Sons. [2]In order to fulfill this special function the Holy Spirit has assumed a dual function. [3]He knows because He is part of God; He perceives because He was sent to save humanity. [4]He is the great correction principle; the bringer of true perception, the inherent power of the vision of Christ. [5]He is the light in which the forgiven world is perceived; in which the face of Christ alone is seen. [6]He never forgets the Creator or His Creation. [7]He never forgets the Son of God. [8]He never forgets you. [9]And He brings the Love of your Father to you in an eternal shining that will never be obliterated because God has put it there.

4. The Holy Spirit abides in the part of your mind that is part of the Christ Mind. [2]He represents your Self and your Creator, Who are one. [3]He speaks for God and also for you, being joined with both. [4]And therefore it is He Who proves them one. [5]He seems to be a Voice, for in that form He speaks God's Word to you. [6]He seems to be a Guide through a far country, for you need that form of help. [7]He seems to be whatever meets the needs you think you

have. ⁸But He is not deceived when you perceive your self entrapped in needs you do not have. ⁹It is from these He would deliver you. ¹⁰It is from these that He would make you safe.

5.   You are His manifestation in this world. ²Your brother calls to you to be His Voice along with him. ³Alone he cannot be the Helper of God's Son for he alone is functionless. ⁴But joined with you he is the shining Savior of the world, Whose part in its redemption you have made complete. ⁵He offers thanks to you as well as him for you arose with him when he began to save the world. ⁶And you will be with him when time is over and no trace remains of dreams of spite in which you dance to death's thin melody. ⁷For in its place the hymn to God is heard a little while. ⁸And then the Voice is gone, no longer to take form but to return to the eternal Formlessness of God.

EPILOGUE

1.   Forget not once this journey is begun the end is certain. ²Doubt along the way will come and go and go to come again. ³Yet is the ending sure. ⁴No one can fail to do what God appointed him to do. ⁵When you forget, remember that you walk with Him and with His Word upon your heart. ⁶Who could despair when Hope like this is his? ⁷Illusions of despair may seem to come, but learn how not to be deceived by them. ⁸Behind each one there is reality and there is God. ⁹Why would you wait for this and trade it for illusions, when His Love is but an instant farther on the road where all illusions end? ¹⁰The end *is* sure and guaranteed by God. ¹¹Who stands before a lifeless image when a step away the Holy of the Holies opens up an ancient door that leads beyond the world?

2.   You *are* a stranger here. ²But you belong to Him Who loves you as He loves Himself. ³Ask but my help to roll the stone away, and it is done according to His Will. ⁴We *have* begun the journey. ⁵Long ago the end was written in the stars and set into the Heavens with a shining ray that held it safe within eternity and through all time as well. ⁶And holds it still; unchanged, unchanging and unchangeable.

3.   Be not afraid. ²We only start again an ancient journey long ago begun that but seems new. ³We have begun again upon a road we travelled on before and lost our way a little while. ⁴And now we try again. ⁵Our new beginning has the certainty the journey lacked till now. ⁶Look up and see His Word among the stars, where He has set your name along with His. ⁷Look up and find your certain destiny the world would hide but God would have you see.

4.   Let us wait here in silence, and kneel down an instant in our gratitude to Him Who called to us and helped us hear His Call. ²And then let us arise and go in faith along the way to Him. ³Now we are sure we do not walk alone. ⁴For God is here, and with Him all our brothers. ⁵Now we know that we will never lose the way again. ⁶The song begins again which had been stopped only an instant, though it seems to be unsung forever. ⁷What is here begun will grow in life and strength and hope, until the world is still an instant and forgets all that the dream of sin had made of it.

5.   Let us go out and meet the newborn world, knowing that

Christ has been reborn in it, and that the holiness of this rebirth will last forever. [2]We had lost our way but He has found it for us. [3]Let us go and bid Him welcome Who returns to us to celebrate salvation and the end of all we thought we made. [4]The morning star of this new day looks on a different world where God is welcomed and His Son with Him. [5]We who complete Him offer thanks to Him, as He gives thanks to us. [6]The Son is still, and in the quiet God has given him enters his home and is at peace at last.

Related Material Available
from Foundation for Inner Peace

THIS SINGLE-VOLUME EDITION of *A Course in Miracles* is available in hardcover $30; softcover $25.

THE SONG OF PRAYER, Prayer, Forgiveness, Healing. An Extension of the Principles of *A Course in Miracles*. Taken down by Helen Schucman in the same manner as *A Course in Miracles*, this twenty-two page pamphlet discusses forgiveness and healing in the context of prayer, contrasting the meaning of true prayer, forgiveness and healing with their opposites. See description following. $3.

PSYCHOTHERAPY: PURPOSE, PROCESS AND PRACTICE. An Extension of the Principles of *A Course in Miracles*.Taken down by Helen Schucman in the same manner as *A Course in Miracles*, this twenty-three page pamphlet discusses the Course's principles of healing and forgiveness in the context of psychotherapy. See description following. $3.

THE COURSE ON TAPE. Forty-two ninety-minute audio cassettes, containing the complete Course, read by Kellie Love, a student of *A Course in Miracles* since 1976. Packaged in an attractive blue carrying case. $140.

CHOOSE ONCE AGAIN. Selections from *A Course in Miracles* in blank verse form. Short, inspirational selections that highlight the beauty of language which illuminates the concepts presented. One hundred twenty-eight pages of personal messages that help turn each moment into a joyous experience. Softcover $8.95.

THE GIFTS OF GOD. The inspired poetry of Helen Schucman, scribe of the Course. One hundred and fourteen poems written over a ten-year period that share the spiritual content of the Course. 144 pages. Hardcover $21.

JOURNEY WITHOUT DISTANCE. The complete inspirational story of how *A Course in Miracles* came to be, taking the reader on a fascinating journey that spans more than seventy years. Meet Dr. Helen Schucman, the highly respected research psychologist who heard a "Voice" dictating the material to her. Learn how Dr. William Thetford, the head of her Psychology Department, aided and supported her. Written by Robert Skutch, co-founder of the Foundation for Inner Peace, publishers of the Course. 142 pages. Hardcover $13.95; softcover $8.95.

Related Material Available
from Foundation for Inner Peace
(Continued)

Video Tape 1: THE STORY OF *A COURSE IN MIRACLES*. A 2¼-hour documentary film available on video cassette. The first half of this memorable film is the inspiring story of how the Course came to be. The second half contains first-hand accounts of over two dozen people who relate how the Course has affected their lives. VHS $60.

Video Tape 2: WHAT IT SAYS. An extraordinary summary of the principal themes in the Course by Kenneth Wapnick, the associate of Helen Schucman, who has studied the Course since before it was published, and who currently leads workshops and seminars on the content of the Course. VHS $50.

Audio Cassette Tape A: WHAT IT SAYS. A forty-minute summary of the principal themes in the Course by Kenneth Wapnick. Identical to the sound track of Video Tape 2. $10.

Audio Cassette Tape B: READINGS FROM *A COURSE IN MIRACLES*. A one-hour cassette of selected readings from the Course. Chosen and read by William Thetford, these readings add a moving dimension to the inspirational and poetic quality of the printed words. $10.

WORKBOOK LESSON CARDS. All 365 Workbook (Vol. II) lessons reproduced on heavy-duty cards, 3¾ by 4⅞ inches, enabling you to carry your current lesson for useful reference throughout the day. $21.

CONCORDANCE FOR *A COURSE IN MIRACLES*. This hardcover volume contains the location of every major word in the three-volume Course, as well as in the pamphlets, "Psychotherapy" and "The Song of Prayer." Each word is shown in context. References are identified by Book, Chapter, Section, Paragraph and Sentence numbers. Available 1993.

Order from Foundation for Inner Peace, P. O. Box 1104, Glen Ellen, CA 95442. All prices include shipping. California residents add 7¼% sales tax.

PSYCHOTHERAPY: PURPOSE, PROCESS AND PRACTICE
An Extension of the Principles of *A Course in Miracles*

Taken down by Helen Schucman in the same manner as *A Course in Miracles*, this twenty-three page pamphlet discusses the Course's principles of healing and forgiveness in the context of psychotherapy. Written for professional therapists, the pamphlet nonetheless will be of help to anyone interested in how the Course's theoretical principle of healing—joining with another through the Holy Spirit—is applied to the field of psychotherapy. Its message is summarized in the pamphlet by this statement: "The process that takes place in this relationship is actually one in which the therapist in his heart tells the patient that all his sins have been forgiven him, along with his own." $3.

Sections:

The Limits on Psychotherapy
The Role of the Psychotherapist
The Process of Illness
The Definition of Healing
The Selection of Patients
Is Psychotherapy a Profession?

The Place of Religion in
   Psychotherapy
The Process of Healing
The Ideal Patient-Therapist
   Relationship
The Question of Payment

L et us stand silently before God's Will, and do what it has chosen that we do. There is one way alone by which we come to where all dreams began. And it is there that we will lay them down, to come away in peace forever. Hear a brother call for help and answer him. It will be God to Whom you answer, for you called on Him. There is no other way to hear His Voice. There is no other way to seek His Son. There is no other way to find your Self. Holy is healing, for the Son of God returns to Heaven through its kind embrace. For healing tells him, in the Voice for God, that all his sins have been forgiven him.

PSYCHOTHERAPY: PURPOSE,
PROCESS AND PRACTICE

FOUNDATION FOR INNER PEACE

THE SONG OF PRAYER
Prayer, Forgiveness, Healing
An Extension of the Principles of *A Course in Miracles*

Taken down by Helen Schucman in the same manner as *A Course in Miracles*, this twenty-two page pamphlet discusses forgiveness and healing in the context of prayer, contrasting the meaning of true prayer, forgiveness and healing with their opposites. The process of prayer is described in the pamphlet as "growth in forgiveness," with healing seen as the affect of the mind's undoing of the belief in separation. This "ladder of prayer" is summarized in the pamphlet this way: "You first forgive, then pray, and you are healed. Your prayer has risen up and called to God, Who hears and answers. You have understood that you forgive and pray but for yourself. And in this understanding you are healed. In prayer you have united with your Source, and understood that you have never left." $3.

Sections:

SONG
OF
PRAYER
Prayer, Forgiveness, Healing

An Extension of the Principles of
A Course in Miracles

FOUNDATION FOR INNER PEACE

So now return your holy voice to Me. The song of prayer is silent without you. The universe is waiting your release because it is its own. Be kind to it and to yourself, and then be kind to Me. I ask but this; that you be comforted and live no more in terror and in pain. Do not abandon Love. Remember this; whatever you may think about yourself, whatever you may think about the world, your Father needs you and will call to you until you come to Him in peace at last.

A COURSE IN MIRACLES is available in the original <u>unnumbered</u> three-volume hardcover set: Volume I, Text, 622 pages; Volume II, Workbook for Students, 478 pages; Volume III, Manual for Teachers, 88 pages. Price for the complete set, including shipping, $40. California residents add 7¼% sales tax. Order from Foundation for Inner Peace, P.O. Box 1104, Glen Ellen, CA 95442.